Feeling spiritually dry or overwhelmed? Step away from the noise and rediscover peace and purpose at the Olive Leaf Retreat. Engage in biblical teaching, heartfelt prayer, soul-stirring worship, and meaningful connections.

Your Hosts

Jenn Dafoe-Turner

Teresa Janzen

Jenn and Teresa recognized a deep longing in women for stillness and connection. The Olive Leaf Retreat was

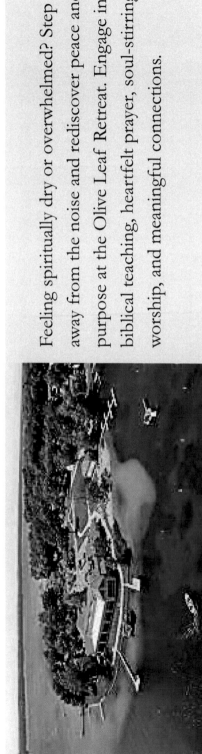

The Olive Leaf

WOMEN'S RETREAT

Refresh, Renew, Re-focus

October 10–12, 2025
Gull Lake Ministries
Hickory Corners, MI

created as a sacred space for women to step away from the noise, be poured into, and hear the gentle whisper of the Holy Spirit.

Speakers Include:

Lora Avery: enjoys discovering fresh Biblical insights and sharing hope and encouragement with others.

Lisa J. Radcliff: Author of *Hidden with Christ: Breaking Free from the Grip of Your Past* and has been teaching in women's Bible studies for over thirty years.

More to come!

What to Expect:

- Inspiring sessions rooted in Scripture
- Intimate times of prayer and worship
- Opportunities for laughter, connection, and healing
- Time to rest, reflect, and recharge

Early Bird Rate: $347 – Ends July 30

Full Price: $397

Spaces are limited—secure your spot today!

Registration Link:

✦ Faith-Based & Purpose-Driven – We align with authors who have a message of hope, encouragement, and transformation.

FREE

Monthly Group Coaching

Show Don't Tell MasterClass

Online Community

Did you know we offer these services?

- AB Publishing Academy
- Writing Buddies
- Speaking Buddies
- Monthly Mindset Group
- La Carte Courses
- A La Carte Marketing services
- Enneagram Coaching
- Strength Finders Coaching
- One-on-One Writing & Speaking Coaching
- Website Development
- Website Hosting and Maintenance

Do you have a book proposal ready to submit?

We accept proposals for fiction, non-fiction, devotionals, and children's books.

Scan the QR code to schedule an interview with our acquisitions editor.

SCAN ME

books@abundance-books.com
www.abundance-books.com

Abundance Books: Shining Light in the Darkness—One Book AT A Time.

Presentened To:

_____

For:

_____

From:

_____

Date:

_____

Endorsements

For ONE CHANCE . . . ONE DANCE

One Chance . . . One Dance offers us a way to express our emotions through movement. It shares those perfect moments of movement that build memories or celebrate the joy of romance, victories, or friendship. Poetry, devotions, and prose combine to share lessons learned through the interaction of the Holy Spirit in our lives' adventures.

~Karen Whiting
Author 30+books, speaker, writing coach

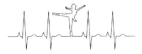

Donna's prose welcomes you into a world of melody and movement! Through her stories and poetry, she paints a portrait of a life brimming with vitality, while Bible verses beautifully highlight each narrative. You'll find yourself captivated as if observing the divine handiwork in a life well embraced. It's truly an uplifting and enchanting literary journey!

~Lee Ann Mancini
Founder of Raising Christian Kids ~Author of Raising Kids to Follow
Christ: Instilling a Lifelong Trust in God
Executive Producer of Sea Kids

If you long to be intentional about living for things that will outlast your life, read this book. Donna Frisinger has given us a unique, personal, thought-provoking, and artistic book. In *One Chance . . . One Dance* she weaves biblical truth throughout each chapter and her illustrations capture the heart of the reader and give take-home value.

~Carol Kent
Executive Director of Speak Up Ministries, Speaker and Author
He Holds My Hand: Experiencing God's Presence and Protection
(Tyndale)

Author Donna Frisinger's *One Chance . . . One Dance* is an inspirational and entertaining book, challenging readers to live in the moment, take the chance, eat the cake, and dance like nobody is watching. Story after story, Donna and several other authors, share their personal and meaningful experiences that will have you laughing one moment and crying the next. But more than anything, you'll be encouraged to leave your comfort zone and shimmy and shine your way through life.

~Michelle Medlock Adams
Multi-award-winning author of more than 100 books, including "Love Connects Us All" "Get Your Spirit On! Devotions for Cheerleaders" and "The Christmas Devotional"

One Chance . . . One Dance is a heartwarming, treasure book of inspirational stories and divine wisdom. Donna Frisinger infuses each page with positivity, encouraging readers to embrace their dreams and dance through life with determination. The delightful poems add a touch of nostalgia, transporting you to a simpler time. This charming book would be a perfect gift for anyone who needs a dose of hope and a reminder of the beauty in life.

~Susan Neal RN, MBA, MHS
Author of 12 Ways to Age Gracefully and Eat God's Food
https://susanuneal.com

One Chance . . . One Dance offers heartwarming stories with biblical application to inspire readers to dance with determination in every trial and trust God in every circumstance. A refreshing read with beautiful storytelling, this book will embolden you to savor the everyday moments of your life.

~Gayla Grace
Writer and Speaker for FamilyLife®, Author of *Stepparenting with Grace: A Devotional for Blended Families*

Hop into Donna Frisinger's toe-tapping *One Chance . . . One Dance* and you'll begin to waltz into joy. Donna's collected stories, art, and inspirations with help you get in step with God.

~Linda Evans Shepherd
Author of *Make Time for Joy, Scripture Powered Prayers to Brighten Your Day*

Years of dance lessons and recitals as a child taught me that dance is indeed an apt metaphor for life. The stories and poems in *One Chance . . . One Dance* form a beautiful collection of reminders of this metaphor. Through the joys and sorrows, victories and trials, the Lord takes us by the hand, choreographs our steps, and leads us in a dance that blesses us and glorifies Him.

~Ava Pennington
Author, Speaker, and Bible Teacher

One Chance . . . One Dance addresses a poignant need for well-being in today's hectic world. As a holistic emotional wellness coach, I wholeheartedly endorse embracing the moments in life. Brilliantly crafted by a team of extraordinary authors, this book is a must-read.

~Tina Yeager, LMHC
Award-winning author, Purpose and Holistic Emotional Wellness Coach, Flourish-Meant Podcast and Flourish Today radio host, and Inkspirations Online Publisher

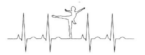

I was pleasantly caught up in the spontaneous rhythm of each story. Though several lives are represented throughout *One Chance . . . One Dance*, the flow of resilience and inspiration had me turning pages with a smile in anticipation of the next dance. Donna Frisinger drew me in with her interludes of perfectly positioned poetry. Each one, in and of itself, swayed me to once again turn the page. Moments are fleeting. The choice to dance amidst each one is up to us. This is a book I'd gladly gift again and again.

~ Linda Goldfarb
International speaker, Award-winning author of the LINKED® Quick
Guide to Personalities series, an award-winning podcaster, and a
board-certified Christian life coach. LindaGoldfarb.com

One Chance … One Dance

Don't Miss the Moments of Your Life

Published by Abundance Books, LLC, Kalamazoo, Michigan, USA
Abundance Books, Ltd., Cambridge, Ontario, Canada
abundance-books.com

ISBN 978-1-963377-02-6(Paperback)
ISBN 978-1-963377-18-7(Ebook)

One Chance ... One Dance

Don't Miss the Moments of Your Life

by Donna Frisinger

Abundance Books

www.abundance-books.com

It's never too late to go looking for those childlike dance shoes to fit them to your feet again and boogie to the beat God. Himself. planted in your heart the day He turned the spotlight of His love on you.

Donna Arlynn Marie Austgen Frisinger

Dedication

This book is dedicated to my past students, who stretched me to become the dancer of dreams that I am today.

It's also dedicated to my fantastic friends, dedicated teachers who read my stories aloud in class, and even the Naysayers—like my college journalism professor who told me, "Girls have no place in the world of Journalism. Change your major."

In retrospect, today, it's easy to see that the venerable Lord of The Dance orchestrated my every step and saved me even in the missteps of my life journey, all contributing to the tapestry of who I am today.

Listen, Earth-Children,
come gather around,
Can you still sing Life's rich
roundelay round?
—Laughter and clapping—
Joy singing in praise,
Dancing new life with the
Ancient of Days.

Contents

I scrub my hands with purest soap,
then join hands with the others in the great circle,
dancing around your altar, God,

Singing God-songs at the top of my lungs,
telling God-stories.

Psalm 26:6-7 (TM)

The Dance of Our Life

"God's got something for me. I have faith it'll be OK. I'm just grateful to be on this planet. I have no enemies that I know of. I'm just the guy who makes happy."
Chubby Checker

Let's Twist Again. The Hucklebuck. The Loco-motion. The Monkey. The Swim . . .

For those fortunate enough to have grown up in the days of *American Bandstand*, the mere mention of certain words conjures up word pictures far from what this present-day generation might imagine. Whereas grandkids might wolf down a mound of mashed potatoes smothered in a lake of chicken gravy, we recall smashing "The Mashed Potato" into our gymnasium floors with the balls of our bobby-socked feet.

Wind that nostalgic clock forward to add protruding Frankenstein arms to those spuds, and we morph into zombie-like marionettes jerked by the strings of "The Monster Mash." And while today's kids squeal amidst tangled limbs to play a game of "Twister," in our minds, we're still drying off our backside with an imaginary towel while Chubby Checker belts out "The Twist."

As babies, we boogied before we could walk, clutching trusted fingers to bounce, bob, march, and sway to Life's music. From the playpens of our living rooms to the aisles of our churches, children dance simply to express joy. And indeed, our Creator smiles as they do.

He is the "Lord of the Dance," after all, and he planted the DNA of our unique life-dance inside each of us. "Before I shaped you in the womb, I knew all about you. Before you saw the light of day, I had holy plans for you . . ." (Jeremiah 1:5 TM).

How we express our life dance is synonymous with our personal story in telling the world about our awesome God and what He's done for us. Sadly, many have misplaced their boogie-woogie as they've matured. What used to be a spontaneous skip — an "I don't care who's watching" happy hip-hop — somewhere along the highways and byways of Life morphed into a drag-your-feet, hang-your-head trudge up a tiring, tedious mountain.

Perhaps you don't even recall when you lost the bounce in your step. We first notice the bee-bop is missing in the faces of our children. For whatever reason, they give up on their spontaneous dance of joy when they get older. Perhaps when they start school.

Like us, they suddenly become aware of the onlookers: Someone might make fun of me. I don't know how to do the latest steps. I don't feel like dancing.

While some of us skip and leap through Life like lambs in a fresh-cut hayfield, others plod the borders of mud puddles when they could be splashing through the middle of them. From sunrise to sunset, with no apparent momentum of their own, they simply let life happen to them. Today, God calls us to rediscover — redirect our steps — to uncover the purpose of our personal Life Dance.

One of the most memorable stories of King David portrays him as recklessly dancing before his God in celebration of the return of the Ark of the Covenant to its rightful place in Jerusalem. As the story goes, in the eyes of his wife, Michal, David got a little carried away. Way over the top, in her opinion, in his undignified dance of grace and gratitude.

Unfortunately, she didn't hesitate to tell him as much, which resulted in her own ruin as the future queen and the mother of untold sons and daughters of the King.

I've often wished Michal had rushed to her husband's side to join him in his dance to make it her own. How might her life, David's life, and the future of Jerusalem and God's chosen people have been different if she had? But she missed the chance to be a kid again, to clasp hands in a circle of merriment to whirl with her king. And don't you know, David would have welcomed her with open arms.

Perhaps you've missed opportunities to dance with the King, serendipitous moments you can never get back. When your own stuffiness, pride, or self-imposed shackles prohibited you from joining in His dance.

I recall with wistful clarity the heat of a sweltering July afternoon when my eight-year-old niece begged me to join her for a spontaneous dunk-and-plunk. Karli had come with me to Culver Military Academy that day to return some costumes I'd borrowed for an Americana musical play I'd directed.

After conquering the swings, monkey bars, merry-go-round, and teeter-totter, with now sweat-drenched clothes and stinging eyes, the near-by waters of Lake Maxinkuckee whispered an invitation to suggest a romp into some good old-fashioned fun. "Hey, Karli," I hollered, "do you want to wade in the water?"

"Can we?" Her blue eyes sparkled, full of youthful excitement, as she looked up into my grin.

"You bet." I nodded. "Come on. Race ya!"

At the water's edge, we took those first tentative steps together, wobbling into a refreshing chill that nipped at the day's heat to gently swirl around our ankles.

"Yikes!" Our shrieks of joy pierced the air like screaming seagulls. Giggling and gasping as Maxinkukee continued its creep up our calves, Karli held tight onto my hand. "This is so much fun, Donna!" she squealed.

I looked down to catch a glimpse of the elf inside her. "Yes, it is, my Karli. Hey, let's march!"

Now, lifting our knees high, the splashing coolness slapped at our knees and thighs, licking at the salty sweat we'd worked up on the playground. Suddenly, Karli dropped my hand to dive head-first under the water, fully immersing herself in the lake's refreshing bath. "Come on in, Donna!" she begged, sputtering in excitement as she resurfaced, "Play with me! You can get your clothes wet!"

She was right, of course. My clothes didn't matter. They'd dry.

However, before this impromptu adventure, I'd just washed and styled my hair that morning. So even as Karli doggy-paddled toward me, I agonized, fighting a wimpy war within my soul . . . until, "Ohhh, Honey, not today, okay? Some other time. We can come back."

Only years later did I realize the folly of my reluctance. I'd missed a perfect opportunity to hoot and holler in a happy-hoopla not only with little Karli but with my King. As you may guess, "some other time" drifted away in the gusty breeze of her growing older, and that precious bonding moment passed me by, never to be recovered.

To this day, I still regret not becoming as a little child that day with Karli. I'll never forget the downcast look of disappointment in her eyes. But as a result, I find myself more willing to throw off the shackles of predictability these days.

Hence, the reason for this book — where I invite you, my readers, to join me and a few of my writing friends in this great adventure called Life, to "dance" with your King. For Jesus himself said, "The thief (Satan) comes only to steal and kill and destroy. I came that they may have and enjoy life, and have it in abundance [to the full, till it overflows]" (John 10:10 AMP).

Maybe you're one of those who's forgotten the spontaneous pirouette of your childhood. Isn't it time to go looking for it? To let go of anything and everything that has crippled your desire to swirl, twirl, and whirl with your Creator.

Bitterness?

Failures?

Heartaches?

Disappointments?

Loss?

Let it all go. Our God is the Lord of a second, third, and umpteenth chance. New chapters are His specialty. And like Disney's Little Mermaid, Arial, our spirits long to dance: "Who says that my dreams have to stay just my dreams. Oh, to dance would be grander than grand. Something inside is daring to try. Daring to sing. Daring to dance."

Life is *waaay* too short, and it's never too late to go looking for those childlike dancing shoes to fit them to your feet again and boogie to the beat God, Himself, planted in your heart the day He turned the spotlight of his love on you.

Tune me into foot-tapping songs,
set these once-broken bones to dancing.

Psalm 51:8 (TM)

No one can dance your unique life-dance but you. To live is to dance! To dance is to live. Jesus is extending His hand. Will you accept His invitation to step onto Life's ballroom floor?

Tick-Tock: Marching Clock

Tick-tock, tick-tock, tick-tock, tick-tock . . .
Seconds counting cadence at conception of a new life
As toothless grins and tottering legs lurch forward on parade
Thru carefree, playful, sun-filled days in rocket-jet-propulsion,
To adolescent toothy smiles in gangly, awkward frames . . .

Tick-tock, tick-tock, tick-tock, tick-tock . . .
Minutes hold their breath in boisterous wonder of excitement
As greasy hair and sweaty brows transform us overnight
To angel girls and muscled boys, first proms, and turning tassels,
Then marriage vows and mortgages with children of our own . . .

Tick-tock, tick-tock, tick-tock, tick-tock . . .
The dunes of the hourglass keep drizzling in a pageant
Of juggling hectic schedules, pacing yard-lines, eight-to-five,
To never-ending meetings, packed-out carpools, paradiddles
Of syncopated "hurry-ups!" that shift to overdrive . . .

Tick-tock, tick-tock, tick-tock, tick-tock . . .
Our days do a quickstep now, as time is strutting faster
From easy tasks we used to do like running after balls,
Or slurping chocolate malts, and eating cheeseburgers at midnight
In guiltless camaraderie *before* cholesterol . . .

Tick-tock, tick-tock, tick-tock, tick-tock . . .
Weeks gliding into months that pinwheel at life's corners
While grasping at fond memories, favorite places, wistful schemes,
We reminisce at class reunion's once familiar lyrics
Of long-remembered tunes that captured snippets of our dreams . . .

Tick-tock, tick-tock, tick-tock, tick-tock . . .
The years stretch to counter-march in pulsing rapid rhythm
As mid-life bulge and graying hair defines *distinguished* brows,
The seasons of our life play tag with bookend generations.
It seems we just mark-time,
yet pages turn—clock's racing on . . .

Tick-tock, tick-tock, tick-tock, tick-tock . . .
Tweet—Tweet, Tweet, Tweet!
The whistle blows a halt to the short decades of our marching
As feeble muscles lose their strength and eyesight slowly dims,
We're helpless babes again who look beyond this fickle drummer
To Eternity's tomorrow where the *tick-tocks* never end.

All-Occasion Cards

"Dance with determination; conquer the impossible."
(Unknown)

I'd discovered the ad on the back cover of one of my Superman Comic Books, one of many popular back in the 1960s. The magnificent three-speed, black, and silver chrome bicycle with the cone-shaped front headlight caught my eye and imagination. At the time, I was riding an oversized, rusty, and hard-to-pedal blue monster that had belonged to my older cousin Patty. My friend, Janie, across the street, had just gotten a blue three-speed, and I was itching for a new bike.

As I quickly scanned the full-page ad, which also pictured many other smaller prizes, I realized that the bicycle was the top prize. All I had to do was sell *two hundred-and-fifty* boxes of "All-Occasion" greeting cards — twenty-five boxes at a time. Piece of cake, right? This was my one chance for a new bicycle since my parents couldn't afford to buy me one with six mouths to feed.

I remember like yesterday the excitement fluttering in my tummy one rainy summer afternoon when the mailman delivered my first order of boxed cards. Before then, I had no idea what "All-Occasion" cards might be. But now, knocking enthusiastically on neighborhood doors, I explained what I was trying to do.

"Hello," I said. "My name is Donna, and I'm trying to earn my dream bicycle by selling these "All-Occasion Cards." Each box includes birthday, get well, wedding, anniversary, new baby, thank-you, and sympathy cards, 30 in all!" I paused to catch my breath before flashing them another smile. "Cards for 'all occasions,' get it?"

Much to my childish delight, they sold like Snickers Candy Bars on a schoolyard playground. In no time, I'd sold the first twenty-five boxes, sent the money order in for payment, and received the next twenty-five. And get this: people were actually thanking me. As it turned out, I was doing these folks a service.

Needless to say, I spent the entire summer of 1962 selling All-Occasion Cards — twenty-five boxes at a time — canvassing nearly every house in Dyer, Indiana, pulling my Red-Flyer wagon piled with card boxes behind me.

However, as the weeks crawled by, it got harder and harder to sell them. I was running out of doors to knock on and had now started canvassing homes in nearby St. John and Schererville, IN. I was often tempted to quit: I could settle for that transistor radio. Or how about the reel-to-reel tape recorder? That pop-up tent would be great fun to camp out in the yard.

But, when I was tempted to "settle," I pulled out that comic book, hidden in my top dresser drawer, to focus on that picture of the black and silver three-speed. And again, my resolve kicked in.

My goal was finally realized, coincidentally, on that Labor Day weekend. As I pedaled the "Blue Monster" to the post office to deposit my final money order, I felt a terrific sense of accomplishment, knowing that my task was complete.

Now . . . I waited on my bicycle.

And I waited.

And I waited.

It seemed it would take forever, like watching a pot of water, waiting for it to boil. The carefree summer days reluctantly gave way to the monotonous rituals of reading, writing, and arithmetic. But finally, one mid-October day, a nondescript cardboard box arrived addressed to me.

But . . . what was this?

Surely, it couldn't be my long-anticipated bike. This package was too small, the size of a baby's tricycle. Had the comic book company run out of the bicycles and sent me something else instead? The small print on the bottom of the ad gave them that right: "Notice: if a particular prize happens to be out of stock, or otherwise unavailable, you may be sent a gift of equal or greater value."

My heart dropped down my stomach and into my shoes. "Oh, no-no-no!" This couldn't be happening.

I wanted that bike.

I needed that bike.

I pictured myself perched on its seat, shifting gears and honking the black bubble horn on that bike.

Mom scrambled up from the basement, her favorite hangout these days. Ever since Dad had lugged the record player downstairs from the living room, she used every excuse in the book to sneak down there to spin her favorite 33 records. She sorted the laundry to Nat King Cole. Crooned along with Frank Sinatra and Dean Martin. Mended clothes on the overstuffed couch, listening to Sarah Vaughn.

"Donna, what's wrong? Did something happen? Are you hurt?"

I shook my head, pointing to the box. "It's supposed to be my bike."

"What?" Seeing my disappointment, she ran to hug me. "I'm so sorry, Honey, they must have sent something else."

"I know," I moaned.

She lifted my chin to look into my tear-filled eyes. "I know how hard you worked selling all those cards. Tell you what, let's see what's inside. It has to be something nice, right?"

I sullenly nodded. "I guess."

We began picking and pulling at the top flaps, glued down tight against the heavy-duty box. "Wait, let me get a knife." She ran to the kitchen.

Once the flaps were loose, I pulled them back to find . . . a pile of junk. That's what it looked like, anyway. "What in the world is this, Mom?"

"Honey . . . I think . . . it's . . . the . . . bicycle."

"What?" I looked at her like she'd lost her marbles. "You're kidding, right?"

"Actually, I'm not kidding." She dangled a plastic see-through sack in front of me. "Look. Here's the nuts and bolts." Then she lifted something else from the box. "This is the handlebar." Now I could make out a black leather seat, and a chain.

Then it dawned on me: This *was* my bicycle. But it was in itty-bitty pieces that had to be put together. Like a giant jigsaw puzzle.

Fortunately, my mechanic-minded dad, co-owner of Austgen's Hardware uptown, had no trouble assembling it.

I'll never forget my happy heart when I laid eyes on my very own, newly assembled, brand-new bicycle—a treasured prize I'd dreamed of and earned all by myself. Me, myself, and I!

As I hopped on the seat for my first cruise, I felt as if everyone in the neighborhood surely must be watching as a happy dance played around my heartstrings:

Satisfaction!

Excitement!

Freedom!

Needless to say, I learned a lot that summer about perseverance and keeping my eyes on a goal, something the Apostle Paul exhorts us to do as Christians. I've often felt like giving up because of hurts, frustrations, and other trials along my life's journey. Many times, I've lost my balance, fallen down, crashed or taken wrong turns to be sidetracked in my purpose by something that looked easier than going after the prize God has called me to.

But today, I ride aboard my cherished retro-look fat-tire, silver and turquoise Schwinn bicycle with shimmering handlebar streamers flying in the breeze, not for any earthly prize but the pleasure of the ride. I put the pedal to the metal to win the applause of Heaven, knowing that Jesus is right beside me to see me through all the "assorted occasion cards" of my life: weddings to birthdays, anniversaries to funerals, sympathy cards to new babies and thank-you's to dear friends who've picked me up after crashes.

But my ultimate goal is to open a special all-occasion card from Him one day to find these words: "Well done, Donna. Enter the place I have prepared for you. You've been my good and faithful Servant. Love, Jesus"

Whatever you do, work at it with all your heart,
as working for the Lord . . .

Colossians 3:23a (NLT)

I greet you with the grace and peace poured into our lives by God our Father and our Master, Jesus Christ. How blessed is God! And what a blessing he is! He's the Father of our Master, Jesus Christ, and takes us to the high places of blessing in him. Ephesians1:2-3 (TM)

Joyride

The sunshine called my name today:
"Hop on your bike, come out to play
While geese are honking overhead,
And bluegills jump the riverbed,
And tree frogs serenade the pond,
As Springtime dips her magic wand."

And so I pedaled on the breeze,
Where songbirds winged from lofty trees,
To soar, no-handed, winding hills,
—A balance act of giddy thrills—
While chasing butterflies that teased
Through Summer's ease, just as I pleased.

My spinning spokes clocked Ferris Wheels
While racing Time on Autumn's heels:
Zig-zagging bunnies froze in frames,
And squirrels played tag in teasing games.
While in cornfields a fawn and doe
Stopped by to watch the tassels grow.

Each new rotation lapped the miles,
Surprising me with Winter's smiles.
The whispering wind combed through my hair
And open roads became a dare . . .
Till shadows lengthened and day died,
Exhaling bliss on Life's joyride.

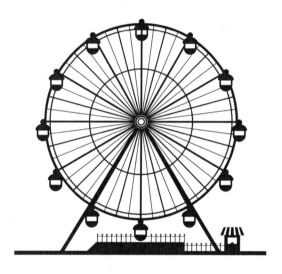

Shoestring Ballet

"I got it!" My tense muscles exploded into an instant running machine at
the crack of the bat. Everything but the small white dot arcing against the
sapphire sky disappeared as I raced toward its rapidly sinking descent from
my post, deep in Center Field. This was it. Now or never. All the hours of
practice and positive self-talk instantly merged into this one brief spurt of
adrenalin rush.

"Go for it, Donna!" My friend, Linda Fryer, was cheering me on from the
infield, the first inning of this championship game. I got the message.

Linda was my hero, the star shortstop of our Dyer, Indiana, "Blazer's"
Girls' Softball Traveling Team. We'd become inseparable that summer,
riding our bikes across town to play burn-out in each other's yards. She
could leap, spin in midair, and chasse to snag the catch with the grace of a
prima ballerina as she scooped up every ball hit within reach from her post
between second and third base. Her seemingly effortless elegance on the
field continued as she'd fire it off to first base as smoothly and *accurately*

as "Mr. Baseball" himself, Ernie Banks, the star shortstop for the 1960s Chicago Cubs and my favorite baseball player.

"Accurately" being my primary emphasis here. For you see, in our untold hours of playing catch, because of Linda, I too learned to "fire the ball." However, my aim could sometimes be more than a little off. Which gave my friend fantastic fielding practice, of course.

Because of Linda's persistence in striving for excellence, my game improved, too. "I want to play in the Olympics someday," she confided to me one winter day over a game of pinochle in her basement. She'd taught me the card game to help pass the snowy winter days while waiting for softball season to start up again.

We'd been paired up on the infield at second base and shortstop for the past four years. That's why it was so shocking when our coach, Hugh Blaze, approached me the spring day before our first practice. "Everyone's hitting the ball harder and farther," he said. "We're gonna need some good outfielders now if we're going to stay competitive. I think you fit the bill, Donna."

Masking my disappointment, I half-heartedly trotted to the distant boonies in center field. Mr. Blaze was like a father to me, especially since my parent's divorce. I didn't want him to see the tears in my eyes.

Now he picked up a bat at Homeplate and began fielding practice, hitting line drives, bouncers, blazing grounders, and fly balls, first to the infield, then out to us second-class clowns in the outfield. At least that's how I felt. Didn't he know a strong infield was the key to winning games? I felt as though I'd been demoted.

To make matters worse, when it came my turn to smother his soaring blow to center field, I'd frantically bolted, only to watch helplessly as the ball flew over my head to effectively poop on my self-confidence. "That's okay, Donna," Mr. Blaze called. "You'll get the hang of it. You just need to learn to read the ball off the bat. Playing the outfield is a different game than what you've been used to doing the last four years."

Now Linda and I set up a new practice routine, spending hours launching muscle-propelled rockets to the sky as we'd go for broke to not let the ball touch the ground before we got to it. Before long, I actually found myself enjoying my new home in Center Field. I could run like the wind, and I found it exhilarating to go after a fly ball and actually catch it.

However . . . there was one little glitch. While I was "Superwoman" at practices, when I'd play in a real game, I'd sometimes psych myself out to suddenly turn into a "Grandma Moses" when it really counted.

Mr. Blaze never got mad at me, though: "Your day's coming, Donna," He'd say. Just keep at it, and one day it'll click."

Right.

I felt like I was letting the whole team down. I'd start after a fly ball, and then, at the last minute, Doubt would come a-knockin': *You're not going to make this catch, Donna. Slow down and take it on the bounce to be safe.* If only I could play as well as I practiced.

Summer vacation whirled by like a swirling polka, a dance familiar to most Lake County residents, many of them of German/Polish descent. The Blazers had enjoyed a winning season, and we were now set to meet our archrivals, the Hobart Blue Devils, in tomorrow night's county championship game.

Mr. Blaze had given the team his usual pep talk ending yesterday's practice. But as I walked from the field to hitch a ride home on my new black and silver three-speed bicycle, Linda ran up to me calling, "Hey, wait up, Donna! Or should I say, 'Time's-up!'"

"Huh? Whadda you mean?" I frowned into her unwavering blazing blue eyes.

"I mean, this is the big one! The county championship!" She hesitated, then continued. "Look, Donna, you're good! You never let a single flyball drop to the ground at practices."

"I know-I know, Linda! I love practices. It's challenging for me to go the distance when there's nothing to lose. But . . . sometimes when I play in a real game, and I know it matters, I just freeze up!"

She nodded, smacking her ever-present softball into her mitt. "So, just pretend you're at a regular practice tomorrow night! I mean, what's the worst that can happen?"

"Yea, but—"

"Look, Donna, you're not gonna win or lose the game all by yourself, right? We've all gotta do our part! Take chances! One play at a time. Fight for what's ours for the taking." She flashed me her distinctive sheepish grin. "And, besides, Mr. Blaze is always sayin' how playing softball is just 'practice for real life,' right?" We high-fived Gloves, and she ran off, calling over her shoulder, "See ya on the diamond tomorrow night. Keep your eyes on the ball. Don't let it hit the ground."

Linda's departing words from yesterday wrapped around my brain, like the last song I'd heard playing on the radio, to repeat over and over again inside my head. I'd thought about her comment all day as I watched the hands of the clock tick-tocking away the hours until, finally, it was time to dress for the game.

As I changed into my red and white Dyer Blazer uniform, buttoning up my jersey, pulling on socks, tying up my tennis shoes, and finally pulling my ponytail through my All-Star Baseball Hat, Linda's final words of encouragement ran the bases of mixed emotions in my mind:

First Base: — *Anticipation:* I felt jittery and hyped up all at the same time.

Second Base: — *Dread:* I didn't want to mess this game up for my team-mates. Going off to college in two weeks, I wanted that trophy to take with me. To remind me of this softball family that I'd come to love.

Third Base: — *Excitement:* This was the championship game. One Chance — One Dance, right?

Finally, I slid home into Determination.

. . . Crack!

Somehow, I'd known the ball was coming my way even before the pitch was released. Before the umpire dusted off Homeplate to call, "Batter-Up!" Before I'd seen the fierce smirk mirrored in my opponent's eyes.

The Blue Devils had runners on second and third with no outs. Any thoughts of a win seemed impossible now. These girls were huge, confident, spirited sluggers, as witnessed in their pregame warmup. Unquestionably, the league's strongest team. In my mind, they seemed like Goliath mocking David at the Valley of Elah.

Now, from my post in deep center, it was just me and that spiraling three-inch leather ball that seemed to take on a life of its own, speeding to drop to the turf, just beyond my grasp. Linda's words of encouragement from yesterday echoed in my mind. *Keep your eyes on the ball, Donna. Don't let it hit the ground.*

I lurched forward, every muscle straining in a dive for redemption. And in that split second, when my glove brushed the grass, I felt a solid *smack* settle into the sweet spot of my fielder's mitt.

Pandemonium!

My seemingly impossible shoestring catch brought the crowd to its feet with a roar, followed by a deafening replay when I continued my forward momentum to accurately fire my captured prize to Linda, waiting on second for the double play.

But wait . . .

She then pivoted to hurl it to third, beating out the player diving headfirst back to the bag. It seemed no one, including the Blue Devil's lead runner streaking for home plate, thought I'd snag that catch.

A triple play!

As it happened, that seemingly impossible shoestring catch ignited the Blazers to victory that night as we all clicked together the rest of the game to hit, run, catch, and dive for impossible fly balls to skippy-do dance our way to the first-ever Lake County Girls Softball Championship.

I still have that trophy in my bedroom today, a nostalgic reminder of my footrace against that ball. A diving shoestring that inspired me to keep my eyes on other goals later in my life, cheered on by great teachers and good friends who saw my potential and challenged me to do my best. Maybe God allows each of us one perfect catch in life to spur us on in the race until we're safely Home.

In a race everyone runs, but only one person gets first prize. So run your race to win. To win the contest you must deny yourselves many things that would keep you from doing your best. An athlete goes to all this trouble just to win a blue ribbon or a silver cup, but we do it for a heavenly reward that never disappears. So I run straight to the goal with purpose in every step.

1 Cor. 24-26 (TLB)

TO-DO List

When life is throwing curve balls,
And I don't know what to do,
I just get out my "To-Do List,"
Checking off each point anew:

___Raise my hands and lift my head up.
___Shout my praises to the King.
___Run into His open arms again
___To lift my voice and sing.

___Open up the Book of Knowledge,
___Seeking wisdom from on high.
___Pray to find some understanding,
___Then I wait on Adonai,

___Holding firm to every promise,
___As I speak the Words of Life,
___Doing battle in my *knower*,
___Not my feelings, causing strife,

___Seeking peace within the chaos,
___Blocking out the frenzied roar.
___There to pour out my devotion,
___And to fly where eagles soar

___In the current of the Spirit,
___Far above my circumstance,
___With my focus on the ballgame,
___Set my heels to take my stance,

___Where I swing to call my pride out,
___ Pounding through the old rundown,
___Slide across the plate of mercy,
___ There to lift the sacred crown.

Skinny-Dipping Lamentation

By Judith Hartzel

"Life doesn't always give you second chances
so take the first one."
Taylor James

We were newlyweds, and it was mid-summer on Cape Cod. My husband, Tom, and I had been invited to attend a concert by the folk-singing trio, "The Limeliters," a performance featuring a newcomer special guest, Ann Mayo Muir, my husband's younger sister. Ann desperately wanted to launch a singing career, and this was her big chance.

Anticipating a formal crowd, I'd dressed to the hilt in my new silky, sheath dress splattered in eye-catching orange flowers. With sparkly matching earrings and bracelet, hair coifed into a French twist, silk stockings, and high heels, I was sure to create a splash. Of course, to ensure my youthful, slim figure didn't dare bulge anywhere, following the crazy trend of the day, I'd also squeezed into a rubber girdle—a torture, no doubt, devised by some crazed man.

Even Tom, usually a casual guy, dressed up in a lightweight navy suit, short-sleeved shirt, and striped tie. As my Sir Galahad gallantly opened the car door for me that scorching night, I noted that not even a slight breeze was stirring.

The sticky-icky air seemed to mock my carefully applied mascara, just daring it to not run off into my eyes. But the unbearably humid conditions didn't matter to us. We were young and in love. And besides, the clubhouse was air-conditioned, right?

The only trouble was that we were mistaken about when Annie would sing, and we arrived 90 minutes early. To our chagrin, we weren't even allowed to wait in the cool air-conditioned lobby because Annie didn't want us to see her rehearse.

Then Tom had an outrageous idea. The clubhouse lay along the shore of a little lake, secluded under a rising moon. We pulled down to the water's edge and turned off the ignition; he eyed me with a devilish grin. "What?" I said.

"Nobody here but us," Tom teased. "I'm going for a dip. You wanna join me?"

"Absolutely not!" I retorted. "You're not serious."

"Oh, I am most serious, Love of my Life. Come on, don't be such a fuddy-duddy." He began to strip off his clothes. "Look around. There's no one to see us."

Before I could adequately protest, Tom ran off to wade into the water. "Come on, Judy, it's so dark, nobody can see us," he urged again. "This feels glorious!"

What was I to do? Go skinny-dipping with him? But I had no towel to dry myself. I thought that if I took off all my tight-fitting clothes, I would never get them back on. And my makeup? My carefully coiffed hairdo would be ruined. I'd have to sit in the car and miss the concert!

So, did I take Tom's cocky dare?

Of course not. Much to my regret today. Instead, I stood forlornly on the shoreline, sulking.

Tom swam for over half an hour, crowing about how delicious the cold water felt. "Most fun of my life!" he hooted.

When he finally splashed from the lake, he walked up to me and shook himself like a dog, intentionally trying to get me wet. "Tom, stop it!" I squealed, to his delight. "You need to get your clothes back on. We'll be late now."

Needless to say, we went to the concert together, one of us deeply content, the other hot and irritated. The "Limeliters" happily strummed their guitar, bass, and banjo, and Tom's sister performed flawlessly.

As you may guess, ever since that missed skinny dip, Tom never tired of teasing me about the serendipitous fun I missed that night long ago: a chance to be a kid again. "You missed it, Girl!" I've probably heard it hundreds of times in the years since.

Now, 64 years, three wonderful children, 5 grandchildren, and three great-grands later, Tom is again swimming in deep waters, this time in the throes of dementia. He doesn't remember that impromptu swim, past golf outings, fun times with the kids, great times we shared, or even that I am his wife some days. He calls me his "mother" more times than not, and if I let myself, I can swim in the currents of despair and sadness today.

But I refuse to live that life of "poor me," as I also refuse to give up on the love of my life. I stay active while Tom sits in front of the TV or works on his jigsaw puzzles, trying to stimulate his mind to read books or sing old songs with me.

Steadying myself with my trusty walking sticks, I try to walk daily, and attend or lead weekly Bible Study at my church. Occasionally, I'll pull out my knitting needles to make a sweater or baby gift, actively enjoying all the new people God has placed in my life's path.

So what would I do differently if I could live Tom's naughty night all again? For one thing, I would have worn loose-fitting cotton clothes, no restraining girdle, and my hair would have been flowing down my back. No stockings, no heels, just sandals on my naked feet . . .

And, I would have taken a towel.

> *When you go through deep waters, I will be with you.*
> *When you go through rivers of difficulty, you will not drown.*
> *When you walk through the fire of oppression, you will not be burned up; the*
> *flames will not consume you.*

Isaiah 43:2 (NLT)

Beach Buddies

Sitting huddled in our beach towels on this blustery, frigid day
Undeterred, we are determined to catch any filtered ray
Wriggling out between the clouds to find this beach on which we lay,
Just two snowbirds, you and I, so let the skeptics hide away

In their claustrophobic chambers, waiting for the sun to shine;
We enjoy this chum camaraderie: time to focus, realign,
Reminisce while telling stories that we've heard a dozen times,
Laugh out loud like little children, yes, but here's the bottom line:

There's a homey old shoe comfort in this escapade we share,
Going all day without makeup, wondering what to eat and where,
Watching sunsets, walking seashores, sharing secrets sealed with prayers,
No commitments cares, or worries, just reclining woven chairs

That have lapped gazillion giggles of "what ifs" and "let's pretend,"
Each memorial in our journey of the years you've been my friend,
With sheer gratitude for blessings, every fond "remember when . . ."
Of the days we've played together — still, beach-buddies till the end.

Boogie-Woogie Bugle Boy

"Dance as though no one is watching you. Love as though you have never been hurt before. Sing as though no one can hear. Live as though heaven is on earth."
Souza

"Hey you!"

The crisp fall air crackled with the smell of newly fallen leaves sprinkled with hints of the dying embers from the Homecoming Bonfire in the field next to my dorm. As I strolled back to my room that evening, swinging my royal blue and white pom-poms, wearing my new "Halftime Honey" dance team uniform, I hummed "*The Butler War Song*," keeping my stride in perfect sync: left—right—left—right . . .

So caught up in the weekend's excitement — the parade I'd just marched, the Homecoming Dance, and anticipating the football game the next day where I'd be performing at halftime — I almost missed that call from behind me.

I hesitated. Was that "Hey you!" talking to me? Glancing over my shoulder and not seeing anyone, I kept walking. Silly. Why would anyone be calling after me? Especially a guy.

Just four weeks into my freshman year at Butler University, even before packing my bags to leave Smalltown America for the big city of Indianapolis, I'd resolved that I would not get involved with any boy. On the rebound from a hurtful high school relationship, nothing or no one would keep me from getting my college degree. I'd heard too many stories of girls abandoning the pursuit of higher education to drop out and get married, and I was not going to join their ranks.

"Yeah, I'm talking to you!" The unfamiliar voice persisted.

Executing a counter-march (a marching band/military term for a sharp "turn-around"), I beheld the image of a perfectly dressed tin soldier standing about five yards away in a Butler University Band Uniform. The feathery white plume, topping his royal-blue box hat, ruffled in the slight breeze as he held his gleaming brass trumpet tight against the white crossbars blazoned across his chest.

I raised my eyebrows. "Me?" I asked, puzzled.

"Can we talk a minute?"

I shrugged. "I guess so."

Striding up to me, his deep brown coffee eyes peering out from behind black-rimmed glasses, the trumpeter steadfastly held my gaze. "Do you want to go to Butler's Homecoming Dance with me tonight?"

Surprised, I balked. "I can't! I mean . . . I already have a date."

Undeterred, Mr. Coffee Eyes continued, an almost imperceptible mischief playing at the corners of his mouth. "Okay," he said. "Well, my name is Barry Frisinger. I think a mutual friend told you about me. That I wanted to ask you out?"

My memory-light finally clicked on as I studied the tiny, pocked scar mark near his upper lip. "Oh, yeah! Carol did ask me if I'd go out with a certain trumpet player friend of hers if he asked. That's you, right?"

Actually, unknown to him, I had seen this guy before when Carol pointed him out to me one day before our noon band practice. The image of a hurried, upright black bear wearing a fuzzy-wuzzy short jacket, racing across the fieldhouse floor that day while puffing on a cigarette — trumpet in one hand, band lyre and flip folder in the other — did little to impress me.

"Please," Carol practically begged me, "just give him a chance. He's really a great guy."

I found out later that Carol's father was the director of bands at Angola High School in Northeast Indiana. He'd groomed this trumpet player standing before me to attend the Jordan College School of Music at Butler, hopefully, to take over his job one day.

Now Bugle Boy relaxed, smiling a crooked grin. "So would you? I mean, will you go out with me?"

I shrugged and nodded. "I guess so."

We made hurried plans to meet for a coke the following Monday at Butler's student union, better known on campus as "The C-Club." After getting to know each other a little that day, he took me to a golf course later that week. Actually, it was a driving range. It turned out that this Barry Frisinger guy could not only make his trumpet croon but could also swing a mean driver.

I've always said that Barry planned that first date so that he'd have to put his arms around my waist to "help me" position my fingers in the correct grip around the golf club.

As for the missed Homecoming dance? Now that's a different story. Let's just say it was the best dance I ever missed because that would have been our one and only date.

Although Barry and I later attended several college sorority dances, we fought at each one. It turned out that although he loved playing music, he hated getting out on the floor to dance to it. So self-conscious, that he imagined everyone in the room staring at him. Waiting for him to fall down? Misstep? Trip himself or otherwise make a fool of himself.

And so instead of holding me close, whispering sweet nothings into my ear, and enjoying the evening, he'd find some little nitpick to complain about every time, even during a slow dance. Forget the fast ones:

"Did you hear the sour note that saxophone just hit?" he'd say.

"Man, that drummer is not keeping up with the band."

"The trombone player is half a step sharp . . ."

Anyway, you get the picture. The only saving grace for us was the making-up after the fight following each dance. It turns out Mr. Trumpet Lips could kiss. Boy, could he kiss! And when he kissed me, nothing else mattered. Four years later, we sealed our lifelong love with that irresistible pucker-up.

But matrimony didn't solve the problem of Barry not liking to trip the light fantastic on a dance floor with me. Not until fifty years later did he find the joy of his own boogie beat.

Unlike our first encounter on that mall at Butler University, tonight, the wind whipped and howled. Pounding raindrops pelted us as we crossed the street to attend a wedding ceremony that would join two of our best friends' children. Shuffling at a snail's pace toward the relief of the carved Victorian Doorway ahead of us, Barry clutched my arm with one hand, holding his scarf around his neck with the other.

I guided him with small, careful steps, not so much for fear of falling but because that was all the faster Barry could walk. Although my husband had recovered well from an open-heart surgery a year earlier, where they'd replaced his aortic valve with a mechanical one, he'd suffered two episodes of a racing heart months afterward.

Medically known as atrial fibrillation, these flareups require a procedure called Cardiac Ablation that uses heat or cold energy to create tiny scars in the heart to block irregular electrical signals to restore a typical heartbeat. Thankfully, he'd had no further problem with fatigue since then.

Until tonight.

I felt so bad for him, a heart-wrenching, crushing ache that only comes after years of loving and caring for the tender-hearted man sharing your bed. Once inside the door Barry tried to put on a good front in greeting old and new friends: "I'm fine," he said. "Just a little tired." But I knew better.

We finally maneuvered to our designated chairs, where he collapsed heavily into the seat. The ceremony, with its simple beauty and the holy atmosphere generated by two families who were crazy in love with Jesus Christ, blew everyone away.

After the bridal meal, traditional toasts, cake-cutting, first-waltz, and tear-jerker Daddy-Daughter Dance, the DJ got down with some serious boogie, playing the latest upbeat Contemporary Christian Music that had the younger crowd whirling and stomping in sassy celebration. The hilarity reminded me of what I imagined the Jewish Wedding in Cana must have been like, where Jesus turned water into wine.

Finally, unable to resist the pulsing beat calling my name, I tugged my girlfriends onto the floor to freestyle and jive. Suddenly, the joyful atmosphere turned into what can only be described as the spontaneous freedom of Heaven hitting Earth. Little kids, teens, young couples, middle-agers, and older couples began jumping up and down like synchronized kangaroos in a contagious, fiercely wild hullabaloo.

Now, wanting Barry to join me, I zig-zagged across the room to where I'd left him talking with the men. "Come on, Sweetheart!" I gently coaxed him from his chair. "Dance with me!"

Unbelievably, he didn't resist.

Holding hands, we navigated the jam-packed crowd of jumping party-goers to find our friends also hopping and hollering, including all the other husbands who'd been pulled onto the dance floor.

Suddenly, in what I can only describe as a bona fide miracle, my previously fatigued, listless, and weakened husband began bouncing up and down, too. And the more he jumped, the freer he danced. Laughing, twirling, and clapping, the shackles that had bound him up for years fell away in one electrifying moment.

I have never felt such joy as when the Holy Spirit descended upon that night's wedding celebration to ignite a true dance of freedom. It was a small taste of what we'll have in Heaven one day when Jehovah Rapha, the Lord Our Healer — the venerable Lord of the Dance — showed up to win over my non-dancing husband.

Fully recovered from all heart disease since that night, Barry hasn't been the same since. He's a regular dancing maniac (at least in the privacy of our living room).

About a year after that wedding, we celebrated our 50th Wedding Anniversary at a small nature preserve in a hall called "The Butler Room," the name reminiscent of the school where we'd found each other a half-century earlier. Coincidence? I don't think so.

And what a blast we had. Twisting, jumping, choo-chooing a conga line, and jitter-bugging with our friends. Especially when the disc jockey played "Boogie-Woogie Bugle Boy," and I caught sight of my Barry "cutting the rug" with our three little grand-nephews who were decked out to beat the band in black derby hats and suspenders.

But my happiness was complete when I felt a tap on my shoulder. I spun around in my red velvet party dress to find my man smiling down at me, the enticing tiny scar near his upper lip still beckoning me. "Hey you . . . !" His eyes sparkled with the same mischief I'd noticed on the Butler Green. ". . . You wanna dance?"

Praise his name with dancing; play drums and harps in praise of him.

Psalm 149:3 (GNT)

Barry and Donna Frisinger
50th Wedding Anniversay

Photo provided by Donna Frisinger

Silver Lips

He works his horn so smoothly, spinning notes of silken wonder,
Crooning tunes as fresh as raindrops chasing after distant thunder,

Soaring to the mountain summits, dipping into somber vales,
Up and down staccato stair-steps, triple-tonguing stunning scales,

Jumping octaves in a symphony of themes-and-variations,
Skipping stones between the written notes in sweet improvisations,

Weaving fantasy and magic with his gift of perfect pitch,
Traveling on a magic carpet ride to mesmerize, bewitch,

Filling cosmos empty spaces with lush harmonies, vibrating,
Fingering heartstrings in a melody to resonate, pulsating

In the shadow of a love-song that it seems I've heard before,
Center-stage, his trumpet sings the strains of Heaven's distant shore,

Playing with an unseen orchestra as myrrh to soothe our souls,
Reminiscing wistful memories stored in homesick cubbyholes,

In a serenade, beguiling, wooing listeners to partake,
Coaxing notes of purest luster only Silver Lips can make.

Adventure in the Rainforest

By Crystal Bowman

"The moment is everything. Don't think about tomorrow; don't think about yesterday: think about what you're doing right now and live it and dance it and breathe it and be it."
Wendy Whelan, American ballet

My husband and kids are adventure seekers. Let me put it this way—I am not. I enjoy many fun activities but usually stay on the safe side of the sidewalk. While they are dashing into the frigid Arctic Ocean for a polar bear plunge, or dropping 52.5 vertical feet down Splash Mountain, I am on the sidelines laughing and snapping pictures with my cell phone. My enjoyment comes from being a spectator rather than a participant.

I enjoy traveling with my family and have been coaxed into some adventures now and then that pushed me outside of my comfort zone—like skiing down a black diamond slope because we "accidentally" rode the wrong chair lift, or going whitewater rafting on what was supposed to be a scenic route. I try to be brave and go along with the majority, but I say "no thank you" when I am terrified of participating.

On one of our spring vacation trips when my college kids had a break, we spent a week in Costa Rica. I had never been to a rainforest, so the experience was educational and enjoyable. We spent hours in the infinity pool, went for a nature hike, and even took an art class where we painted the beautiful scenery. But it was our excursion on the last day of our trip that made my heart beat a little too fast.

My husband, Bob, and the kids talked me into joining a group of tourists that signed up to go zip-lining. "It's so much fun!" they said. "You will love it!" they assured me. And so, I stepped aboard the minibus and rode for more than an hour deep into the heart of the rainforest.

When we arrived at the site, we were given a helmet and a harness. So far so good. Then we followed the guides and trekked up a stone stairway that continued for longer than I expected. Up, up, up, we went. I was glad I wasn't the only person panting and slowing down as we ascended the steep hill. When we finally reached the top, I made the mistake of looking down. We were higher than high, and I started to panic.

"I'm not going to do this," I whispered to Bob. Before he could answer I asked one of the guides how I could get back down. "The only way down is on the zip-line, Ma'am," he explained. "And we have a couple of repels plus a Tarzan swing. It's a blast!"

Bob saw the fear in my eyes and assured me it was safe. "You'll be fine," he said. "You can do this."

If it was possible for me to get out of this zip-line adventure, I would have done it in a second. But there was no way out, so I had no choice. My heart beat rapidly and my body trembled as the guide clipped my harness to the bar that was attached to a wire line. Then he gave me a push that sent me zooming toward the next platform. I tried not to look down and focused straight ahead so I would not be aware of how high I was. For some reason, my body turned around and I began racing backward, fearing I would smash into a tree. I soon came to a stop where another guide grabbed me and unclipped my harness. I stood on a narrow wooden platform attached to a tree and waited for the rest of my crew to join me. Did I mention I tried not to look down?

"Are you okay?" asked Bob as he arrived on the platform. I nodded. "That wasn't so bad," I said as I took a few deep breaths. And just like that, I was attached to another zip-line for my second ride. I was a bit calmer this time, but my body still turned backward as I sped toward the next stop, and I could not see where I was going.

Once everyone completed this round, we zipped again from platform to platform a few more times. One of the guides told me to pull my knees to my chest, which kept me facing forward so I could see when I was coming to the end the line. "I'm starting to enjoy this," I told Bob with a smile. He looked relieved.

Just when I was getting comfortable with the zip-line routine, we came to a platform that didn't have any lines—just a long rope. "You need to hold the rope tightly and swing from this platform to that one," said the guide as he pointed ahead.

Once again, I was on the verge of a panic attack. The guide sensed my fear, clipped my harness to the rope and told me to hold on. "You're going first, Mama," he said as he pushed me off the platform. Before I knew it, another guide grabbed me and held on to me until my feet were safely planted.

After another Tarzan swing and a few more zips through the trees, we were finally reaching a lower elevation. At another station, the guide taught me how to repel to continue our descent. For some reason, I wasn't afraid to try that, and I was surprised at how well I could physically manage it.

After one last zip-line we finally reached the end of our adventure and walked to the cabin to return our helmets and harnesses. The guides offered us a cool fruity beverage as we waited for the bus to pick us up. I had a small blood stain on my shirt and had no idea how it got there or where it came from. "It's your badge of courage," said Bob as he put his arm around me. "Good job, Mom," added my kids who were sincerely proud of their non-adventurous mother.

We posed for the typical tourist photos, then rode the bus back to our hotel. After a warm shower and some local cuisine, I felt a great sense of satisfaction and accomplishment because I had done something I was terrified of doing.

It's been more than a decade since my zip-line adventure in the rainforest. As I have reflected on that experience many times, I am reminded how I need to trust God when I am afraid. Just like those narrow platforms kept me in a safe place, and just like those guides cared about helping me, God protects me and cares about me even more. God's love and protection are far greater than a wooden platform or human hands. God is with me all the time, no matter where I am and no matter what I'm doing. And whether I am struggling physically, emotionally, or spiritually, He is strong when I am weak.

In Psalm 46:1, the psalmist writes, *God is our refuge and strength, an ever-present help in trouble.* God is the One I can turn to again and again, even when I can't see where I am going, or when solid ground seems too far away. He is the One I can hold on to when life is fragile. And he is the One who holds on to me when I am terrified.

"For I am the LORD your God who takes hold of your right hand and says to you, Do not fear; I will help you."

Isaiah 41:13 (NIV)

In The Woods

In the woods
I know your presence,
In the woods
I see no wrong,

In the woods
I feel your heartbeat,
In the woods
I hear your song.

In the woods
we walk together,
In the woods
you hold my hand,

In the woods
I taste your goodness,
In the woods
with you I stand.

In the woods
all fear is banished,
In the woods
I sing your praise,

In the woods
my thoughts are gathered,
In the woods
my hands are raised.

In the woods
we talk of glory,
In the woods
my heart is cleansed,

In the woods
I am your child,
In the woods
we are best friends.

In the woods
I touch creation,
In the woods
your blessings flow,

In the woods
you hear my secrets,
In the woods I slow . . .
I grow.

Dancing In Oz

"You have to love dancing to stick to it. It gives you nothing back, no manuscripts to store away, no paintings to show on walls and maybe hang in museums, no poems to be printed and sold, nothing but that fleeting moment when you feel alive. It is not for unsteady souls."
Merce Cunningham

Tweeeet!
The shrill blast of the whistle cut through the crisp autumn air like a newborn's wail. *"Stop-Stop-Stop! Get Donna Austgen off the field. She's making everyone else look sick!"*

It was 1967. I was nineteen, a sophomore at Butler University, and although I'd made the Halftime Honeys Dance Team as a freshman, this year I'd been chosen as one of two alternates. The existing rules said I could perform only if one of the regulars could not.

I'd been heartsick after the audition results were announced. Didn't they know I'd already been sucked into a terrible twister and subsequently slam-dunked to the ground earlier that morning? All I'd been trying to do was change my major from Journalism to P.E.

My trek into the Land of Oz began when the Wicked Witch of the West traded in her broomstick that day for a sharp pencil to harass me and send me staggering down the yellow-brick road to Butler's College of Education Center. As I sat, looking at my watch — I had dance team tryouts in one hour on the other side of campus —it seemed I'd been waiting forever when the secretary finally called my number.

As I handed my transfer papers to the cantankerous spinster drumming her gnarled fingers against her desktop, my nerves were dancing a ragged tap dance. With her glasses pulled down over her crooked, hooked nose, her ratted black tresses nearly covered her beady eyes.

She snatched the forms from my hands, glanced over them, and then screeched, "Why in the world would you want to do a stupid thing like this?" Everyone stopped to stare.

"Because . . . I want to," I squeaked. *Was that a cackle I heard.*

"Well, you'll have to go see Colonel Baron, the head of the Journalism Department, to get his okay." She threw the papers back at me.

And so I was off to Emerald City, first to see the mayor of Oz, Colonel Baron, then onto three more stops through an agonizing poppy field of questions, a murky forest of interrogation (Lions and tigers and bears, oh my!) and dodging flying monkeys of second thoughts.

Finally, I followed the Yellow Brick Road back to the Wicked-Witch, who, with minimal prodding, soon had me in tears: "You'll be sorry, my pretty!" I wished I had a bucket of cold water to throw over her.

To say my self-esteem had been shattered by the time I arrived at my dance team auditions at twelve noon was an understatement. As if I weren't already wholly off-balance, to make matters worse, I'd just started my period that morning and was definitely feeling the fatigue of tip-toeing through my personal, unwelcomed red poppy field. Who could think straight, let alone compete in a grueling tryout for one of the sixteen spots on the Butler Dance Team?

In retrospect, the results had been predictable. I'd stumbled over my own ruby-red slippers in my attempts to spin, jump, smile, and snap. "I'm just going to quit," I told my trumpet player boyfriend later that day. "This is *soooo* humiliating. An alternate?"

Barry put his arms around me and drew me close, a response that would have typically set my heart to racing. "I don't blame you, Honey." He kissed my forehead. "I'd probably want to quit too. I'm so sorry."

I'd picked Butler in the first place because it was home to the only college dance team in Indiana at the time. My high school band director, Doug Jordan, had told me about the famous "Halftime Honeys" as I prepared to graduate, my senior year in high school.

The marching band's pom-pom corps had been my passion throughout high school. With that knowledge in hand, when my guidance counselor took me and three other kids to visit Butler University that fall, I'd quickly decided the prestigious Indianapolis campus was my perfect "Somewhere Over The Rainbow."

I remember being so nervous that first day at tryouts, arriving starry-eyed, fresh from the cornfields of Dyer, Indiana — the proverbial model of Small-town USA. As I entered the gates of Hinkle Fieldhouse for the first time that day for auditions, I knew I was definitely not in Kansas anymore.

These girls could dance! I mean, really dance. In addition to its basketball program, Butler is still well known for its prestigious dance school. Starry-eyed teens came from all over the country, hoping to make it big in the world of dance.

Although I'd been part of arguably the best high school marching band in Indiana at the time, most of my dance experience had been relegated to high-stepping pom-pom routines. Still, I clicked my heels together and put my best foot forward that day.

When I found my name prominently displayed first on the "Sweet 16 List" posted on the front door of the Jordan College Hall of Music the following day, I squealed in delight. Okay, so my last name began with an A, which accounted for its prominence at the top of the list. But still, my dream had come true. I was a bona fide Halftime Honey.

Now, a year later, bidding goodbye to my boyfriend, I walked back to my dorm room, dejected. How could I stay on the squad if I never even got the chance to perform? It didn't matter if I did a better job or worked harder than anyone else. The only way I'd perform was if someone got sick or hurt. Fat chance.

That night, I cried myself to sleep. But somewhere in the middle of my heartache, I decided I would not quit. No. I would prove them wrong.

And so I worked hard. Every single time I went through a routine, I tried to make it better than the last time. I still didn't perform.

I never missed a rehearsal. In fact, I arrived early.

I still didn't perform.

I never complained and smiled to beat the band.

I still didn't perform.   And then . . .

One fateful autumn day, my dance team captain, Karen Talley, approached me before practice: "Donna, I need you to take Sarah's spot today during band rehearsal. She's sick."

Finally!

I sprinted to the fifty-yard line, and I did my thing.

We were three-quarters of the way through that rehearsal when Butler's wiry band director, Mike Leckrone, blew that piercing whistle to yell through his megaphone from his perch, high on the hillside that over-looked our practice field: "Karen! Didn't you hear me? I said, 'Get Donna off the field. Now! She's making the rest of the girls look like amateurs!'"

My heart thudded against my chest like a trapped bird. Outwardly, I stood perfectly still, at attention, barely breathing. But inside, I was smiling as wide as the whole hundred yards.

Oh, I still didn't get to perform. Sarah was back the next day. But it didn't matter anymore. The Wizard had noticed me! He'd stopped the whole practice to let me — and the entire band — know it, too.

That band director, Mike Leckrone, went on to direct the Big Ten University of Wisconsin Marching Band. Me? I was voted Captain of "The Halftime Honeys" my senior year. At that time, I changed the policy of "no-challenge alternates."

After graduating, I married that trumpet player boyfriend of mine, and together, we went on to direct several state-champion high school marching bands and dance teams. In 2005, I was named the Indiana State Dance Educator of the Year and later co-founded the IHSDA — Indiana High School Dance Team Association — which is still going strong today.

I could have quit that pivotal day long ago. I could have played the blame game. Claimed tryouts weren't fair. The odds were stacked against me. Stopped when the going got tough. I've seen too many girls play the role of the Cowardly Lion in my years of coaching. But even though my Scarecrow brain tried to tell me I didn't have a chance, fortunately, my Cowardly Lion heart wasn't ready to give up on my dream. I had a choice to make: to give up — or get up. And that choice has made all the difference in my life.

Over the years, I've found nothing that cripples my ability to dance through this life more than my inability to let go of negative feelings. Like Dorothy in Oz, however, I've learned the only road home — the path to true success, peace, and contentment in God's Kingdom — lies in throwing a bucket of cold water over my personal antagonists: self-doubts, imaginations, bitterness, un-forgiveness . . . to then click my ruby-red slippers, pick myself up, and try again.

As Norman Vincent Peale once said, "If you want to get somewhere, you must know where you want to go and how to get there. Then never, never, never give up."

Once again I will rebuild you. Once again you will take up your tambourines and dance joyfully.

Jeremiah 31:4 (GNT)

Dance Children Dance

Let the children dance, Let them flourish, skip and sing. Let the children dance, Let their tender hearts take wing. Let the children dance, Let them run to Christ our King.

To Dance Again

Sparkling dancing waters,
Amidst the ebb and flow,
Like diamonds cast by God's own hand
To shimmer, skip and glow

Upon the dark blue surface
That covers up the deep
Unknown, foreboding, hidden world
That interrupts my sleep.

For hidden there beneath this cloak
Of rippling, peaceful calm,
Lie gaping fissures of despair
In need of healing balm.

So I present my offering
To Him Who knows my needs,
Who sees the buried chambers:
Strings of rotting, tangled beads.

And only I can dredge them up
To see the light of day,
To cleanse the hurt and heal the pain:
Release me, Lord, I pray,

Please cast me on these waters,
To reflect the Son above.
To dance again, a precious gem,
In Your amazing love.

courtesy Donna Frisinger

May I Have This Dance?

by Pam Farrel

"When you dance with someone, you allow yourself to be vulnerable and open. You have to trust your partner, and in doing so, you create a physical and emotional bond."
Julianne Hough

Dancing with each other has been a part of our love affair since our early dating days. Bill and I have been happily married for over 44 years, and we like to think we waltz our way through life's ups and downs. For us, it is a natural response to linger in one another's arms where our hearts beat together as one. Like a passionate Tango, dancing and romance can be a beautiful pair to fan the flame of love.

Famous dancing genius Fred Astaire once said, "In Dancing, two people become one. You must trust your partner, let go of your inhibitions, and work together to create something beautiful." That's Bill and me: our love affair has been, and is, something beautiful. We've intentionally woven the fine art of dance into our love life. We danced at our rehearsal dinner, our wedding, and our wedding night. We believe in building "Romantic Moments" into our daily lives and dance anytime we wait for an elevator.

My grandparents square danced every Saturday night of their 60+ year happy marriage. Even though Bill and I only occasionally square dance or line dance, we've worked to follow the example of those loved ones, who would even two-step together each time they met in the kitchen.

Intentionally dancing our way through life as best friends, we've noticed that dancing together in public most often gives us the opportunity to explain the source of our love: God. We even dance down the frozen food aisle in the grocery store and regularly silly-dance while waiting for fast food, which once led to the cashier asking us the secret to our long-lasting love. We talked to her about the love of God, and the next time we came in, we brought her one of our marriage books, which led to us connecting her and her fiancé to premarital training.

Each Saturday in the summer, there is a concert in a park near the marina where we dock our live-aboard houseboat where we often dance on the bow. To most in our marina, we are known as "that dancing couple." And we love it.

Did you know that even Science backs up the insight of the world's distinguished dance professionals? A study published in the *Journal of Couple & Relationship Therapy* found that couples who participated in a 12-week dance program experienced improvements in relationship satisfaction, communication, and emotional closeness.

The Archives of Sexual Behavior also found that couples who participated in regular partner dance classes reported higher levels of relationship satisfaction (including sexual pleasure) than those who did not participate in said classes.

In addition, another study published in the *Journal of Dance Medicine & Science* found that dancing can effectively reduce stress, raise positive endorphins, and increase feelings of well-being. According to the experts, a daily walk hand-in-hand by a couple could be followed by a nightly dance around the bedroom.

In my newly released devotional book, *Growing a Joyful Heart* (co-authored by Karen Whiting), I share more benefits of dancing:

- It releases happy endorphins.

- Creates natural painkillers.

- Boost the adrenaline system, creating energy.

- Releases pent-up tension and lowers stress.

- Bolsters brain health.

- Improves coordination and confidence.

- Enhances overall physical health.

- Enriches balance and spatial awareness.

- Develops social skills

Martha Graham once said, "Dance is the hidden language of the soul." Named "Dancer of the Century" by *People* magazine, she was the first creator of modern dance to devise a truly universal dance technique out of the movements she developed in her choreography. "My dance language," she said, "was intended to express shared human emotions and experiences rather than merely provide decorative entertainment," a truth my husband and I can attest to today.

One particular "dancing date" stands out in my memory today. We were on a cruise celebrating our 25th anniversary and had just taken our lives into our hands to try a zip line course to fly above cares and life's problems. Then, upon returning to the ship for a refreshing dip in the pool and shower, we'd enjoyed a triple date with friends over dinner with an ocean view, then walked hand in hand under the stars in the sand.

As we strolled along, we suddenly became aware of an unexpected tune floating above the serenity of the beach. So, we followed the sounds and ended up in the city square to find a live band playing. Under the strings of lights woven in the palm trees overhead, we danced in the enchantment of our unexpected discovery.

Then, knowing our time on shore was drawing to a close, we strolled back to the ship to slow-dance under the stars on the upper deck to the music of the ship's band. As fireworks from the shore lit up the sky above our heads, Bill leaned in and whispered, "Let's just say I planned this all for you."

We both giggled as we continued dancing, wrapped in each other's arms, knowing beyond a doubt that God our Father had orchestrated our dance steps that evening, even as He'd taught us the essential steps of unity and closeness in our beautiful marriage.

What Is A Friend?

What is a friend if not *Truthful*?

A fellow poet casting garlands of pearls, yet fainting not at spewing pellets of stones in good faith—even when they hurt—who understands small nuances hidden in replies that mask your deepest feelings.

What is a friend if not *Faithful*?

A fellow climber clinging to that last knot on the rope beside you, cheering you on, encouraging you to hang on when hands are blistered, muscles strained and weak, and all you want to do is let go.

What is a friend if not *Uplifting*?

A fellow clown inducing gales of tummy-tickles, refurbished at remembering the yesterdays of better times: nonsense songs, spontaneous dance, gourmet foods, and first romance.

What is a friend if not *Compassionate*?

A fellow priest lending an empathetic ear, straining to reach out with calming arms of care to embrace silent tears forever stored in trustworthy confidence in reservoirs of Hope.

What is a friend if not *Prayerful*?

A fellow express-rider delivering your latest request through rain or shine, with tenacity and timely speed, carefully affixing the stamp of their personal "Amen" to forever seal it in Heaven.

What is a friend if not *Hopeful*?

A fellow artist painting the best possible portrait of people and events, trusting that all things will be used for good to complete the now imperfect picture of my life. Not a Picasso, but a Michelangelo.

What is a friend if not *Helpful*?

A fellow builder jumping in with rolled-up sleeves to be the needed hands and feet of the Master Architect, following His blueprint, seeking not the limelight, but only to lay the next brick.

What is a friend if not *Spontaneous*?

A fellow traveler out to see the world through childlike eyes, dreaming and scheming to make Joy happen, wasting not a minute in idle chatter or stagnant thought, but moving ever forward in delight.

What is a friend if not *Gracious*?

A fellow troubadour singing sweet harmony, enhancing my melody strummed by angel choirs, comfortable in their role upon life's stage. Costumed in robes of silken blessings, cotton service, and linen grace.

What is a friend if not *my* friend?

A fellow sojourner traveling upon this sod, only passing through to Kingdom-Come, a Smiley-Face painted just for me by The Creator's caring forethought upon the canvas of my life.

A Special Delivery

"She had to dance —she just had to! The music seemed to move in her body,
moving through her. She leaped high and flung out her arms and
oh, how she smiled!"
Amy Ehrlich

This was ridiculous. Of course, the local dime store wouldn't carry burgundy leotards. But I was desperate. I needed one, and I needed it now.

As Rochester High School's Dance Team director to thirty-some teenage girls, I was used to playing Mom and taking care of last-minute emergencies. Whether it was a missing button replaced by the quick fix of a safety pin, picking up a student who needed a ride, or running to retrieve a prop some darling dropped in the hallway ten seconds before the halftime buzzer, I prided myself on being able to handle any crisis they threw my way. Once or twice, I'd even been known to peel off my T-shirt, dance pants, or shoes to give to some girl who'd *accidentally* forgotten hers at home.

But a burgundy leotard presented an impossible challenge. I'd ordered the unique Valentine bodysuits and matching leg tights months ago from one of the many dance uniform catalogs stacked in the band room office. One of the girls' mothers had volunteered to make the sparkly pink wrap-around skirts to complete their unique Valentine's outfits for tonight's show. We were 45 minutes from tip-off.

Sophomore Pam Zimmerman had come charging down the school hallway in a panic earlier that day: "Mrs. Frisinger! Mrs. Frisinger! I need help! I can't find my burgundy bodysuit! I've looked everywhere for it!"

"Everywhere?" I asked, shaking my head. I knew these girls. They were forever losing things — or claiming someone else had taken something because "I left it right here!"

"Everywhere!" Pam bellowed. "Even under my bed! What am I gonna do, Mrs. Frisinger?"

Ever the drama queen, she was in tears, close to hyperventilating. "Calm down, Pam," I confidently reassured her. "One of the other girls probably just picked it up by mistake. It'll show up, I'm sure. We'll ask the team at practice after school today."

But the rehearsal had come and gone, and still no burgundy leotard. Which is why I now found myself at our small town's only department store, frantically scanning the underwear aisle in search of the impossible. Unbelievably, I'd just located a small pile of black leotards and was frantically digging through them to see if perhaps —"

"May I help you?" The sales clerk had apparently noticed my rummaging and, in order to keep me from entirely destroying her tidy display, figured she might want to help me out.

"Yes," I said. "I'm looking for a burgundy leotard."

"I'm sorry," she huffed, straightening the pile even as we spoke. "All we have is black. We've never carried any other colors."

"I know," I groaned. "I was just hoping —"

"Well, hope all you want. But you're not going to find a burgundy leotard here." She smiled weakly and hurried off to take care of a more prevalent problem at the sound of a clattery crash followed by the shrill scream of a howling toddler.

I bowed my head to pray: "Lord, I know this problem is not very important in the big scheme of things going on in the world right now. But you know I really need a burgundy leotard, and I need it now! If I don't come up with one, Pam won't be able to perform tonight, and all of our formations and spacing will be messed up. The girls have worked so hard on this special Valentine Show. You are the God of Impossibilities. Could you please provide me with the impossible?"

I finished with a sigh. I'd done everything humanly possible to come up with the leotard. I'd checked the "Lost-and-Found" at school, called every mother, scoured the dressing room three times, combed through lockers, and pleaded with girls. Now, I opened my eyes and started to walk away.

But wait!

What is that?

Sticking out from underneath the counter, on the floor?

A scant smidgen of something . . . burgundy?

It couldn't be. Could it? I reached down to tug at the wine-colored cloth, my heart pounding. As I stood, it skipped a beat to pitter-pat into a triumphant cadence of joy. I couldn't believe my eyes. It was a burgundy leotard! A size "medium," too, just what I needed. I hadn't even thought to tell God I needed the burgundy leotard in a medium.

I shrieked and started to giggle — loudly — hooting hysterically.

Customers clamored to see what was happening, scrunching eyes and whispering, shrugging and pointing at me. The saleswoman rushed back to my side. "What's wrong? What happened? Are you okay?"

As I raised my arm to reveal the burgundy bodysuit, I doubled over, a country creek spilling down my cheeks as I cried tears of joy. "Thank you, Lord! Thank you, Lord . . .!"

"Bu... bu... but we don't carry burgundy bodysuits!" she stammered in disbelief.

"I know! I know! But God owns a whole warehouse full of them!" She looked at me like I was crazy.

I was.

Crazy in love with a Creator so concerned about my piddly little needs, he'd sent an angel down to drop off a medium-sized burgundy leotard to Small Town, USA, plopping it right where I could see it.

"I'll take it!" I hooted as I tossed her the leotard, racing to the cash register. "Hurry. I've got to get to the game before halftime!"

Panting and flushed, I dashed into the band room. The dance team was dressed to perform and was now on the floor stretching out. Pam stood to one side in tears, dejected. She wore her black leotard in hopes I might let her perform that way.

I wrapped her in a cuddle hug. "Pam, you know I can't let you do that. You'd stick out like a cricket among a cluster of ladybugs."

"I know, Mrs. Frisinger." She sniffled, swiping at the liquid disappointment leaking down her rouged cheeks. "I was just hoping — *hiccup!* — and so were the girls —"

"But..." I cut her off, plucking the brand-new burgundy leotard from my dime store sack, "... I can let you dance in this!"

Her eyes bugged out, and her mouth dropped, for once speechless.

"Oh, Mrs. Frisinger!" one of the dance team girls yelled across the room. "You found Pam's bodysuit!" Everyone clapped, screaming, and squealing as they jumped up and down.

I waved my hand to silence them. "No! I didn't find it, girls. But God had one burgundy leotard special delivered to Rochester, Indiana, tonight."

Tugging off the price tag, I handed the new burgundy leotard to Pam as I told everyone the incredible story, ending with, "Well, don't just stand there, Girl. Go get changed! And hustle!"

Rochester's State-Champion Dance Team did a top-notch job that evening. I was sooo proud of them. And as they ended in their finale bring-down-the-house kick-line, I caught Pam's eye to wink. The smile plastered across her face reached the rafters.

I grinned up to Heaven. "Happy Valentine's Day, Lord. I'll never forget your special Valentine's gift to me today. You are just way too cool!"

Keep on asking, and you will receive what you ask for. Keep on seeking, and you will find. Keep on knocking, and the door will be opened to you. For everyone who asks, receives. Everyone who seeks, finds. And to everyone who knocks, the door will be opened.

Matt. 7:7-11 (NLT)

Ending Like Sha-Bam!

Prologue: Stage Fright:

Drinking in a long, slow breath of life,
Every muscle strains in anticipation.
My puny bladder aches with the pressure of nervous fabrication
As I purse my lips, feeling the gloss of lipstick.
Panic! What if I mess up?
Or I can't remember!

Rehearsals:

Point! Turn out. Dig deeper. Lunge.
Plia'. Level change. More energy!
Spot. Spin. Stick-it! Think ahead. Watch your spacing. Smile!
Counting off measures. Over and over and over . . .
Just one more time,
Once again . . .

Performance:

Then, suddenly, the music starts
And the here-and-now converges
With all the yesterdays of sweat, aching muscles, impatient practices.
We work together. She is part of me.
She is doing her best.
Am I?

Finale: Applause:

Now we are one, moving in sync,
Grooving to a living, pulsing beat.
And I celebrate this dance, this rush, getting-down with my friends,
Giving everything, and all I am to stretch
toward excellence; ending like
Sha-bam!

Walk The Line

Will they notice me?
Do I want them to?
Maybe yes . . .
Maybe not . . .
I don't know . . .
Walk the line.

Will they laugh at me?
Do I make the move?
Should I smile,
Stare ahead,
Play pretend?
Walk the line.

Will my outfit work?
Do I look the part?
Am I stylin' . . .
Too glitzy . . .
Just, right?
Walk the line.

Will they hang with me?
Do I talk to them?
"How ya doin'?"
"Nice shoes!"
"What's up?"
Walk the line.

Will they like my hair?
Should I straighten it?
Get it layered,
Or scrunch it?
Go pink?
Walk the line.

Will they think I'm weird?
Do I think they're cool?
Maybe yes . . .
Maybe no . . .
I am me!
Walk the line.

Dancing In The Eye Of The Storm

By Amanda Forster Schaefer

"We can't choose the music life gives us, but we can choose how to dance to it."
Unknown

I remember feeling paralyzed. I can't count how many times I had gone into the bathroom to cry that day, running the water so my children wouldn't hear me sobbing. I wasn't sure how much more I could bear.

Outside, the snow continued to fall. It was one of those heavy, wet snows. The kind that strains your back when you try to shovel it. We had already gotten three feet, and I wondered how much more would accumulate throughout the night.

The air was bitter and sharp, not the best combination with all that snow, making the roads impossible to navigate. I felt trapped. My heart was as heavy as the icy drifts outside my window. Were things ever going to change? At that moment, I had no faith that they would.

I had been praying, begging God to move, but it felt like my prayers only lifted as high as the ceiling, quickly falling back down upon me. Where had God gone? Wasn't He supposed to always be with me?

As if the day hadn't been hard enough, my husband was drinking again, and we were all stranded in the house with him. I prayed that he would pass out and leave us alone. "Please, Lord, I need peace," I whispered with my last breath of hope.

I went to the couch to scoop up my new puppy, Maybelle. Holding her made the moments feel bearable somehow. Her tiny body was warm, and her wet nose tickled me when she kissed my cheek and nose. I felt deeply grateful for this reprieve.

Snuggling her tightly against my chest, suddenly, I could tell something was wrong. She squealed, and I looked to see what was wrong with her. Oh no! Her face was swollen and bumpy. It looked like it had looked when she caught the honeybee flying too close to her the first week we brought her home.

"What happened to you?" I said in my sweetest mama voice. "It's winter; what could have bitten you?" I asked as if she were able to answer me. The children were asleep, and I was alone in the living room with her.

She began to tremble.

"Benadryl!" I shouted out loud, surprising us both. That's what the veterinarian told us to give her before. I ran into the bathroom and got it from the medicine cabinet. I remembered we had to cut the pill in half because she was so tiny.

I got a sharp knife from the kitchen drawer and cut along the score line on the bright pink pill. Next, I grabbed some bread and rolled it into a ball. Maybelle didn't like to take pills, but she loved bread.

The fear that had taken me by surprise began to subside. What would I have done if we were out of Benadryl? I thanked God that we had some. Maybe he would hear my prayer of gratitude. A prayer of thanksgiving, rising from a season of struggle and pain. Yes, there were still good things in the world. And I knew it.

I picked Maybelle up and held her over my shoulder like a newborn baby, swaying and gently patting her back. As I hugged my darling puppy, I whispered my love to her while we danced in circles around my living room to a silent sonata.

Outside, I could see the snowflakes were still falling. It was both beautiful and terrifying all at once. To be stuck in that place with no escape. "Don't worry, everything will be fine," I cooed.

As we twirled in circles, I caught a glimpse of myself in the mirror across the room. There I was, patting and consoling my puppy, just as I wished to be comforted.

And then she started to gasp. I hugged her closer. Her heartbeat seemed to be as slow as her breathing. Something was definitely wrong. What was happening? "How could you do this to me, God?" I yelled in desperation.

Then, a thought: *I must have given her too much medicine!* "Oh, no! Is this really how this night is going to end, God?" The vet's office and the roads were closed, and now my heart was closing, too.

A startling *bling* broke the tension and silence. Jumping, I picked up my phone to see a text from my friend Barb. She lived around the corner. We went to church together. "Can I come over?" the text read.

She wants to come to my house. Now?

I sat on the couch with Maybelle in my lap and responded. "It's 'snow-mageddon' out there, Barb!"

"Yes, now! I have to. It's important."

What in the world?

"Okay. Honk when you get here. And please, be careful," I texted back.

Honestly, the interruption had calmed me, and now Maybelle seemed to be calm, too. "Oh, thank you, God," I whispered as I raised my chin toward the ceiling, imagining my words rising to him. "I guess maybe she is okay after all." I began to breathe normally again.

"Whew, that was so scary," I told her. "I love you so much, Sweetie!"

Bling!

Barb texted me that she had arrived. "Come on out here," it said.

She wants me to come outside? You've gotta be kidding!

"It's freezing out there!" I typed, "And I definitely don't want to come outside!"

"You have to come out here," she wrote back. "God said so!"

What?

Reluctantly, I grabbed my winter coat. The one that made me look like Santa Claus, red with a white fur hood long enough to reach my ankles. I put Maybelle on the couch with a blanket, and she immediately curled up into a fluffy ball.

I stepped outside.

To my surprise, the evening was quiet and peaceful. The snow swirling through the air and the halo from the lamppost reminded me of a scene from Narnia. "Wow! This is beautiful, God." I trudged to Barb's car.

"Hello!" we both said as she got out and wrapped her arms around me tightly, hugging me like she'd never let me go. "Everything is going to be alright," she whispered, patting my back like I did with my puppy.

Then . . . she pulled me into a slow circular dance right there in the snow. Glancing down, I thought our footprints looked like a waltz tutorial — left, right, left, right, turn. . . .

"Barb," I finally said, "Why are we hugging and rocking back and forth in this crazy dance? It's one a.m., and we're in the middle of a snowstorm!"

With a shaky voice, Barb squeaked, "I hope you don't think I'm a weirdo, but God told me I needed to come to you. To slow-dance in circles. Hug you, and rock you. To pat you on the back and tell you everything will be alright."

Tears streamed down my face. They felt warm against the frosty air as I told her what was happening at home with my husband and the puppy. "Thank you, Barb. And you're no weirder than me. I mean, look at us!"

We giggled like schoolgirls. Barb was among the few friends who knew what I was going through. She had dealt with someone in addiction as well and had been praying for our family.

"You are a blessing to me tonight," I said, swiping at tears as our impromptu dance ended.

Out there in the still quiet of the night, dancing in the eye of the storms that raged around me, God had sent me this angel to comfort me, precisely as I had been comforting my new puppy so I would know He had sent her.

How amazing is God? Every detail matters. Every prayer is heard. Even those that feel like they never left this world to reach Him.

That night, He reminded me that He lives in my heart and knows my prayers before I even speak them. The Bible says that I am never alone, no matter my feelings.

By the time Barb left, she was crying too, tears of hope and healing.

Standing there in the silence by myself, I began to dance again. I don't think I have ever felt as loved. As seen. Or as heard as I did in that very moment, dancing in a hushed white wonderland with my God.

You have turned my mourning into joyful dancing. You have taken away my clothes of mourning and clothed me with joy,

Psalm 30:11 (NLT)

A friend loves at all times. Proverbs 17:17a (ESV)

Moonlight Promise

Golden Orb, you cast your spell
Upon this rippling water,
A spotlight chasing doubt away
From Abba's weary daughter.

The sparkling mantel that you've spun
From teardrops of this day,
Reveals a glittering net now cast
To float in tranquil bay.

My soul is soothed by whispering leaves
That crown these ancient trees:
"Come dance with me, my precious child,
Soar on refreshing breeze.

"For shimmering on this peaceful mirror,
Aglow with times and names,
Reflections of the passing years,
One constant still remains:

"Though shadows pounce from every side
To whisper their cruel lies,
You know that your Redeemer lives,
The Promise never dies."

A Red Carpet

"Chase your dreams. Let your dance be the path to success."
Unknown

The dazzling blonde could have been a super-model as she glided onto the stage of my life to part the crowded dance floor like Moses commanding the Red Sea. "Donna," she said, "God wants me to tell you that He's laid out a red carpet for you. But, unlike the typical celebrity runway, this rug is stretched out before you in every direction. You can't make a wrong turn because His hand of blessing is upon you."

My husband and I were guests at a wedding reception some 400 miles from home. The bridegroom, the only other person we knew that day, had asked me to be his "stand-in mother," his own parents not being allowed to attend their son's wedding due to their crippling religious doctrine.

Reminding me of a 1970s princess, dressed in her empire-waist turquoise gown, the woman continued speaking as if I were a long-lost friend, her vivid robin-egg blue eyes piercing my soul. "So don't fear making a mistake, Donna," she continued. "Your talents are gifts from God. He knows your heart's desire to use them to touch people's lives for His Kingdom. To give them hope. His hug. A new song to sing."

"I'm sorry," I shook my head, wracking my brain to remember if I should know this mystery lady, "have we met before?" I glanced behind me, looking for my husband chatting with the bride and groom. Perhaps he knew her.

"No, you don't know me." She smiled, closing her eyes and shaking her head. "However, you do know God, and He knows you, Donna. You've been hurt. You're discouraged and disappointed. Dancing in a circle of self-doubt. But He wants you to know He loves you and has rolled out his red carpet before you."

There it was again: Red Carpet?

But wasn't a red carpet reserved for royalty? For visiting dignitaries and heads of state? Movie stars up for an Academy Award?

As if reading my mind, she whispered into my ear. "Remember, Donna, God is for you. There's nothing you can do — or not do — to disappoint Him." Then she turned to float back through the crowd, leaving me open-mouthed with tears pooling.

"Who was that, Donna?" I jumped when Barry, who was also staring after the enchanting vision, walked up behind me.

"I have no idea," I answered in awe. "An angel?"

How did she know? How could this stranger possibly understand and voice the assurance I needed to hear today as I struggled with my life's vocation?

From little on, I'd worked hard to overcome the taboos of a broken home, striving to block out the memories of sexual abuse at the hands of my grandfather, not to mention the stigma of pooping all over myself — and my desk — in the fifth grade. In my ten-year-old mind that dreadful day, it seemed that the white-collared woman shrouded in black enjoyed the power she held over me in denying my all-consuming need.

Not once.

Not twice.

But three times after wobbling forward, squeezing my buns to ward off the coming tragedy. "Sister, may I please use the restroom?"

"You know the rules, Donna." Like a dark-eyed hawk looking down at me with a superior glint in its unmerciful eyes, she continued: "You will go when the class goes."

Ultimately, my "really have to go" diarrhea explosion overruled her tidy timetable that day.

I remember squirming within that warm icky glob, swiveling my head every which way like the rest of my classmates who were sniffing the air, trying to locate the source of the putrid odor. Maybe they won't know it's me, I naively thought.

Fat chance

Even sixteen years later, while teaching fifth grade myself, I routinely told students at the start of every school year, "If you need to use the restrooms, you can do so at any time. No permission required."

But, even as I taught in the classroom, my overriding passion peculated in coaching my band director husband's auxiliary dance teams, where we paired up to "Wow!" audiences on football fields, basketball courts, and state and national competitions. Not far into this rollicking adventure, we also joined forces to march with Jesus Christ for the rest of our lives, sharing our new hearts in traveling the state with our Christian Music Ministry before helping to pioneer the Faith Outreach Center Foursquare Church, in Rochester, IN.

Now, I found myself directing children and adults alike to share God's love through the performing arts. Dance teams, vocal groups, swing choirs, musicals — each production bigger and better than the last.

Always a stickler for excellence, I made a point of sharing my life's mantra: "If you're going to do something in the Lord's Name, you need to do it with excellence!"

But recently, it seemed like the windshield wipers swiping across my life's windshield had rusted into a nerve-raking *skreich*. I was "wiped out," my creative energy tired of constantly thinking about the next show. Each one, bigger and better than the last.

Every new production inevitably ended with some insensitive soul asking, "How you gonna top that next year, Donna?" Although I'd chuckle, my laughter felt forced lately, my "get-up-and-go" tank running on fumes. Yet, never one to quit anything, it seemed the Lord had always had to knock me up the side of the head to get my attention, as in "It's time to turn the page."

Oh, I'd prayed like a scratched record stuck on the same refrain: "Father, is there something else you want me to do?" But the heavens remained brass, and my hollow pleas never seemed to penetrate beyond my own half-hearted knocking.

Shortly after what turned out to be my last hurrah, my pastor's wife, who knew of my inner turmoil, approached me one day: "Donna, would you fly to a "Dare to Dream Conference" in Anaheim, California, with me? The church will pay our way."

"Duh!" I accepted the invite.

But, while the speakers proved inspiring, the sessions stimulating, and new friends accepting, as I listened to other's dreams for the future, my soul cried. Sitting there in a comfy padded pew in the anything-is-possible "Land of Disney," I found I had no dream. Only confusion and emptiness. My previous passion? Non-existent.

As the conference wound down, the leader surprised us: "Today, ladies, I want you to write a letter to God, laying out your future goals, hopes, and dreams. We'll mail your self-addressed envelopes back to you in six months so you can see how God has answered your prayers."

I walked to a far corner and wrote:

Dear Lord,
I guess I'm doing what you want me to do. And if this is all there is, so be it. I willingly lay down my life to your will. But, if it's not your plan for me at this chapter in my life, please help me to turn the page. To open the next door. And give me the grace to close this one.
Love, Me

With that prayer of relinquishment penned and sealed, I returned home with a renewed will to continue doing the work I believed the Lord had called me to. Bloom where you're planted, right?

But then the Great Deceiver blindsided me when the proverbial carpet of fate was yanked out from underneath my dancing feet. And it wasn't a red carpet either, but a raggedy rug reminiscent of my fifth-grade fiasco. Some pervert had told people my student's dances were "vulgar and suggestive," even comparing one routine to "pole dancing!"

Huh? What in the world was pole-dancing?

When my pastor explained, I felt humiliated and hurt. I'd always taken great care to make sure my choreography was fun. Joyful. Vibrant and life-lifting. Why would anyone say such a nasty thing?

Now, reprobate tongues, misunderstandings, and knives of despair twisted into my thought life, carving out chunks of blame, bitterness, and unforgiveness. Only later did we discover this dirty-minded bearer of lies was plugged into pornography.

I quit. In the process, disappointing shocked students, parents, and a community that loved my work.

As therapy for my broken heart, I started writing down my thoughts and feelings. At first, my musings merely provided a therapeutic release to deal with a festering hurt. But then, after daily cruising the countryside on my "retro-look," white-walled, fat-seat Schwinn bicycle, my mind switched gears to notice otherwise insignificant prompters of memories.

A traffic sign triggered an almost life-ending day during Driver's Ed, my sophomore year in high school. A pile of empty paint cans sparked the pain of blistered fingers from hand-rubbing oil chalk into murals for my Junior Prom. A barking dog tripped the unforgettable heartache of the day when Mom said, "Donna, will you take Beauty (my childhood German Shepherd) to the vet to be 'put down?'" Or whatever else might trigger some flash from the past.

Amazingly, I now found myself enjoying my "Bicycle Reflections," as I now called them, and my fingers itched to get to my computer after each day's ride. I'd started college as a Journalism Major before switching to Elementary Ed, the kid whose stories teachers read as examples of "good writing." Could the Lord be calling me back to my first love? And then . .
.

One prophetic day, my friend and church secretary invited me to go with her to a writer's conference snuggled in the rolling serenity of the Blue Ridge Mountains. I readily accepted, and while there witnessed God's hand go ahead of me in such miraculous ways that I still shake my head in wonder today. In directing my steps to the "right" classes, I met the contacts I'd need for my inspirational musings and children's stories as God opened up a new world of possibilities for me.

To top it off, upon returning home from that writing conference, my "Dare to Dream" letter, I'd written to God six months earlier, waited for me in my mailbox. As I read my own words, I shook my head in amazement. God had, indeed, closed one door to open another. He'd even added in a bonus at the final awards ceremony at Blue Ridge when they called my name as the "First-Place Poetry Winner" for my entry "Sandpiper Hopscotch."

I floated back to my table that night, accepting congratulations from class instructors, magazine editors who'd asked for submissions, and possible book publishers. Holding my award certificate against my chest made me feel like a movie star who'd just received the Academy Award. A Grammy! The Nobel Peace Prize! For, indeed, my soul finally *felt* at peace.

But I would be remiss in not revealing the further surprise God had in store for me when I pulled back my chair that night at the Blue Ridge Conference to catch a glimpse of the carpet. It was red.

"You did not choose me, but I chose you and appointed you that you should go and bear fruit and that your fruit should abide, so that whatever you ask The Father in my name, he may give it to you."

John 15:16 (ESV)

O Lord, our Lord, how majestic is your name in all the earth! You have set your glory above the heavens. Psalm 8:1 (ESV)

Sandpiper Hopscotch

Sandpiper hopscotch, jumping over waves,
Hip-hop, hippy-hop, twiddle tummy craves

Tiny, tasty tidbits sure to satisfy your beak,
Flit-flit-flitting in your game of hide-and-seek,

Chasing the receding tide to scurry back to land,
Tick-tock . . . racing time across the shifting sand,

Fleet-footed, toothpick legs seldom stop to rest,
Flit-flit-flitting — running from the rising crest.

Sandpiper, bitty bird, forever on the go,
Blip-bop, bibby-bop, darting to-and-fro,

Always in a tizzy dip, digging on this strip,
Flit-flit-flitting as you turn to flirt and skip,

Playing tag to dance a jig upon this peaceful beach,
Plip-plop! *Plunky-dunk!* Do you ever reach

An ending to this silly game of playing cat-and-mouse?
Flit-flit-flitting . . . sun and sky your open house,

Created by the Maker of the Ocean and the Sea,
Sing-song winging hymns of praise that shout, "I'm free!

To *skittle-skattle-skuttle* in the wake of His salvation,
While *flit-flit-flitting* to the God of all Creation!"

Shall We Dance?

By Michelle Medlock Adams

"Marriage is not a ritual or an end. It is a long, intricate, intimate dance
together and nothing matters more than your own sense of balance
and your choice of partner."
Amy Bloom

Since our oldest daughter, Abby, was getting married that June, my husband Jeff and I decided it might be a good idea to take some dance lessons because we knew there would be lots of dancing at the reception, and we really didn't want to embarrass ourselves — or Abby. Now, if you know me, you know I love to dance. I was even on the highly competitive dance team—the "Starsteppers" — in high school. But dancing with a partner is quite different than performing a choreographed group routine.

And even though Jeff and I had been "dancing" together since we were high school sweethearts, we had never really danced very well. We grew up in the 80s when swaying side to side to Chicago's "You're the Inspiration" and Lionel Richie's "Truly" was totally acceptable. No fancy twirls, complicated steps, or dramatic dips. Just swaying and holding each other tight.

Sure, we always had a good time, but we truly had no idea what we were doing. We knew it was time for some professional intervention, so we called upon one of the best in the industry: Ms. Kathy. She had owned Kats Dance Studio in our hometown for many years, and we were confident she could help us master a few key steps for our daughter's very important day.

We showed up to that first class with a few nerves, but Kathy soon assured us that we were among friends. And, as it turned out, we were! We knew all but one couple in that class, and everyone was so supportive. And, thankfully, most of them were from our generation —swayers, not swingers.

That night, we took our first steps down the ballroom dancing path, along with seven other couples. And though Jeff and I certainly were not the best in the class, we enjoyed just being in each other's arms while looking into one another's eyes for 45 minutes.

Over the course of the next few weeks, we learned some Salsa, Swing, the Foxtrot, and the basic Waltz. We definitely made progress with each class, but we were no Fred and Ginger . . . more like Fred and Wilma. Still, we were having a wonderful time on the dance floor.

But dancing wasn't all we were learning — not by a longshot.

One night, after a few weeks of instruction, we had the entire class laughing because Jeff picked me up and pulled me where he wanted me to go on the dance floor, loudly proclaiming, "Woman, let me lead!"

Apparently, in my enthusiasm to get the steps just right, I had taken over "the lead," which had us bumbling and fumbling all over the dance floor. While it was a humorous moment for everyone else, it was also a teachable one for me.

Our amazing and accomplished dance teacher stopped the music, smiled, and said: "Ballroom dancing is enjoyed the most when it is done correctly. With the man leading very strongly and the woman following his lead . . . the same way God has intended a man and woman to live together in this world. This makes the unit so enjoyable for the participants and to those observing."

I think every man in the room said a hearty, "Amen."

Jeff pulled me in for a big hug and said, "See, you gotta let me lead!"

He was right, and so was Kathy.

Jeff is the spiritual leader of our home, and I respect him with every fiber in me, but sometimes in my overzealousness, I try and take the lead, and everything gets out of whack. Just like our dance became ugly and confusing on the dance floor when I took the lead, our marriage lacks harmony and ease when I become "Tammy Takeover."

Truly, life is so much sweeter when we do things God's way, right? Ephesians 5:25-33 clearly tells us that husbands are to love their wives as Christ loves the church and that wives are to respect their husbands. This passage of scripture has gotten a bad reputation in some circles, but it shouldn't be perceived as a negative message. Rather, it's the recipe for a happy marriage.

The Word always works!

When our husbands love us the way that they should, and we respect them as Christ commanded, we can move through life as one, and it's a beautiful dance. I'm so grateful that Jeff and I have been doing this dance of life together for almost 33 years, and it just keeps getting better and better. Now, our ballroom dancing? Well, let's just say that Fred and Wilma are in need of more lessons.

For husbands, this means love your wives, just as Christ loved the church. He gave up his life for her to make her holy and clean, washed by the cleansing of God's word. He did this to present her to himself as a glorious bride without a spot or wrinkle or any other blemish. Instead, she will be holy and without fault. In the same way, husbands ought to love their wives as they love their own bodies. For a man who loves his wife actually shows love for himself. No one hates his own body but feeds and cares for it, just as Christ cares for the church. And we are members of his body. As the Scriptures say, "A man leaves his father and mother and is joined to his wife, and the two are united into one." This is a great mystery, but it is an illustration of the way Christ and the church are one. So again, I say each man must love his wife as he loves himself, and the wife must respect her husband.

Ephesians 5:25-33 (NLT)

Hummingbird Tango

Teeny-tiny twittering birdie, dancing your life's tango,
with fairy wings a-fluttering faster than my beating heart,
split-second daring pivots as you spin upon a sunbeam,
to pirouette and hover in mid-air before you dart

first left,   now right,
                  then forward

                    back
in pulsing rapid-rhythm,
flirting and seducing as in giddy first romance,
retreating just before the kiss—a fickle lover's caper,
maneuvering for the set-up, dangling in hypnotic trance,
            Till suddenly . . . a
     zip   *zap*
        zip
into a patch of crimson,
for dipping into sugar cones to guzzle nectar's bloom,
while drinking deep in satisfaction, resting from your caper,
a slivery, slurping, straw-like needle serving as your spoon.

One Stroke At A Time

by Barry Frisinger

"Golf is deceptively simple and endlessly complicated. It satisfies the soul and frustrates the intellect. It is at the same time, rewarding and maddening. And it is without doubt the greatest game mankind has ever invented."
Arnold Palmer

I was one putt away from victory, paired with the self-proclaimed but undeniable powerhouse golfer of Steuben County, Indiana. It had been touch and go for the past nineteen holes of this critical match-play, the final round at Zollner Golf Course in Angola, IN. At only 5'3", I must have looked like David facing his Goliath to my worthy opponent, Doug Smith, who was no doubt willing me to miss this putt.

As I set my stance, a squawking squadron of Canadian Geese flew overhead in their typical V-shaped formation, honking to beat the band and disrupt my concentration: *"You're gonna miss it — miss it — miss it…"* Their sassy sing-song seemed to mock me and my chance of winning that day.

Don't get me wrong. At age 25, with the cocky confidence of youth, I felt calm, capable, and confident, self-assured in my own game. My high school golf coach hadn't nicknamed me "Mighty-Might" for my size alone, but for the unexpected mighty blasts off the head of my clubs on the fairways, precise chip shots around the green, and my ability to read the greens for putts.

Still, I'd missed the 20-footer on today's eighteenth hole, which would have effectively sealed my victory.

Now, Doug and I were in a hole-by-hole "sudden-death" fight to the finish, the Club Championship on the line. We'd tied on the nineteenth hole to send us off to number twenty.

Now, standing with my feet set shoulder-width apart, I eyed what I hoped would be the winning putt. Coming into the hole, I'd hit a decent shot off the tee to land just short of the green. Doug must have overcompensated, blasting his high-riser over the pin, then chipped on and missed his putt to bogie the hole.

After going through my ritual routine of pretending to toss a baseball underhand to determine how hard to swing, my ball landed a mere foot away from the flag. But experience had taught me this supposedly easy "clunk" into the hole was just far enough away to carelessly miss. And, in that moment, I thought about my dad, who'd missed his dream of becoming a professional golfer.

Ralph Frisinger wasn't my biological father but had adopted me as a package deal when he married my divorced mother. I was four years old, and I adored him. Everything about him.

Everything he did. Including his love for the game of golf.

As a toddler, he'd let me ride on the back of his cart when he played with his friends, sometimes handing me a 7-iron to let me swing at the bitty ball. But more often, it was a putter on a green. And then, when I turned ten, he surprised me and bought me my own set of clubs.

After that unexpected gift, every spare minute would find me on the golf course: dodging raindrops, playing blind man's bluff in the fog, sweating bullets under a summer sun, or shivering icicles in late fall. I lived to play the game my dad loved. The game that I now loved.

I remember like it was just yesterday when I looked up from a putt on the second hole at the Lake James Golf Course to see my mother running up the fairway, panting like a water-starved mama bear as I watched —in shock! — on the green.

What in the world?

Upon reaching her goal — Me! — Mom grabbed my arm and shouted, "Barry Lee Frisinger! Did you think you could just go off and miss your trumpet lesson today by hiding out on the golf course? Not on my watch, Buster!" I cringed, embarrassed in front of my golfing buddies, but Mom won the tug of war in my heart that day. I'd just started trumpet lessons, and she wasn't about to let me off the hook. Today, I thank God for a mother who made me practice because Music was to be my life's vocation.

It was about this time that I found out my dad had won the "Michigan State High School Golf Championship" in 1939. Ralph had desperately wanted to play professional golf after finishing college, but his wealthy parents had denied him that dream after only six weeks on the tour.

With only a handful of exceptions, like the great Byron Nelson, Sam Snead, and Ben Hogan, golf in the mid-1940s wasn't exactly the reputable game we watch on our Big-Screen TVs today from the comfort of living room couches and reclining chairs. Many of its players were

considered ruffians, boozers, and brawlers. Besides that, it definitely did not pay out the big bucks that today's top players take for granted, giving Dad's mother and father more than enough ammunition to crush his dream.

In the game of golf, as in real life, there are no "do-overs." No friendly "Gimme's" or Mulligans off the tee if you dub your first drive. You can't say, "Aw shucks, that one stunk. I'll just hit a new ball," because it's the only game in the world where you, yourself, are competing against yourself. Your own conscience. Your personal sense of honor.

There's no cheating, nudging the ball one way or the other to get a clearer shot at the hole. No unlimited foul balls off the bat, as in baseball. No second chances to hit the bullseye or kick the football again to send it spiraling between the goalpost. Strictly adhered to, golf truly is a "Gentleman's Game." So my dad bowed out and sacrificed his dream, going on to other things.

First, there was Pharmacy, as his parents had wished. But feeling no satisfaction in filling prescriptions, Dad set about chasing the American Dream to become an entrepreneur. Over the course of his life, he purchased his own car dealership, a beer distributorship, the first car wash in town — and finally, just a few years prior to his death, his own Century 21 Real Estate Business.

He told me toward the end of his short 62 years of life on this earth that he wished he'd discovered the real-estate gig from the get-go because he found joy and genuine satisfaction in helping people purchase their perfect home.

Meanwhile, his passion for the game of golf trickled down to me and later to my younger brother. I'd been chosen to play varsity golf as a freshman in high school and could have excelled at the game if I'd dedicated myself to practicing the long hours. However, both my band director and my golf coach teased me relentlessly, saying, "Lyndy-Lou stole Barry's lips *and* his follow-through" (Lyndy, being my high school girlfriend).

All of this played in my mind as I stood over the ball on the 20th hole of the Match Play Championship that day when a robin's twittering song snapped me out of my reverie and back to reality where I was one putt short of victory. I took my stance, placing my putter firmly behind the ball to line it up with the suddenly marble-sized hole in front of me. Then, slowly inhaling, in that moment of truth, I moved my putter about two inches back away from the ball, paused, and held my breath while executing a perfect pendulum follow-through to tap the ball.

Plunk!

I had my first club championship under my belt.

The following summer, I collected another club championship trophy at the rival Lake James Golf Course across town. The same course where my mother had drug me off to my trumpet lesson that memorable day in the springtime of my youth.

By the way, I would be remiss if I didn't mention that I took my college girlfriend, now my wife of fifty-three years, to a driving range on our first date. I've seen God bless me time and time again, not only with Donna but with goodhearted friends who've come alongside to chip, putt, bogie, and birdie my life's golf courses. The most recent is my new best friend, Jeff Shelburne.

Although I barely knew the Shelburnes at the time, Jeff and Jeannie had waltzed into my critical care room the day following my open-heart surgery in Fort Wayne, Indiana. "We came to pray for you," Jeff said.

We'd bumped into each other occasionally through the years, but the only thing I knew about them that day was that they'd been involved in music ministry throughout most of their married life, much like Donna and me. I also knew Jeff was a fellow trumpet player.

Two years ago, Jeannie died of Covid.

Jeff was lost, suddenly missing his lifelong playmate. His prayer partner. His best friend. When I asked him to play golf with me later that summer, he hedged. "Oh, I'm not very good. Haven't played a lot — just once a year when my church sponsors a one-day tournament." He paused with a negative shake of his head. "You'd go to sleep on the fairway waiting on me."

But with an encouraging, gentle shove from both me and my wife, he finally conceded: "Okay, but don't expect a Tiger Woods to show up. I'm bad."

From that first round until today, we've paired up to talk and walk the fairways at least once a week, sometimes more. This past summer, we hit the links fifty-five times and actually won Jeff's church outing.

As I've often told my people, I've had two grand passions in my life, other than my dear wife: playing my trumpet and golfing, and Jeff is now part of both. Today, he's lost over fifty pounds and counting, taking at least ten strokes off his original score. But more importantly, Jeff and I are now best buddies — there to hug, cry, plan, advise, and pray together. My all-time favorite player, Arnold Palmer, once quoted Ecclesiastics 3-4 this way,

> *"There is a time for everything, and a season for every activity under the heavens: A time to be born and a time to die, a time to plant and a time to uproot, a time to kill and a time to heal, a time to tear down and a time to build, a time to weep and a time to laugh, a time to mourn and a time to dance, . . . and a time to GOLF!"*

Mirror Of God's Word

Mirror-Mirror, in my hand,
Treasure of God's perfect plan,
Clearly show me who I am,
Sought and bought by Heaven's Lamb.

Clearer-Clearer, may I see
Snapshots of your Truth for me,
Flashes of redeemed esteem,
Freed to live to Faith's extreme.

Nearer-Nearer, bathed in Grace,
Draw me to The King's embrace.
Looking-Glass of God's own heart,
Now unveil your work of art.

Hula-Hoop-Hoopla

Take a hula-hoop and pull it up to your waist,
Swirl it all around and hula,
Round and round, and round and round . . .
Hula, hula, hula — hula hoop!

From my ankles to my knees, up my waist, chest, and neck, 'round one arm, then the other . . . I could keep that hoop spinning with nary a drop back when I considered myself "The Queen of Hula-Hooping." It was a time when kids ran free, jumped ropes, played catch, rode bikes in the street, and kicked the can until lightning bugs flashed and mothers called from open screen doors, "Time to come in and take your bath!"

Then, if you were lucky, a bedtime story, prayers, a goodnight kiss, and "I love you," before snuggling under crisp clothesline-dried sheets, while high in the sky, outside our bedroom windows, the moon would finally whisper, "Goodnight."

Today, those hula-hoops have returned once again, along with bell-bottomed pants, mood rings, flowered hippie tops, and "Prairie Dresses" inspired by the "Granny Dresses" my generation wore. At my high school, in my sophomore year, they even held a special "Granny-Dress Dance!" I still have that dress today, although there is no way I can fit into it. But I do take it to my class reunions . . . on a hanger.

I have an entire closet in my basement, filled with 1960s Dyer Central High School memorabilia that my former classmates depend on me to bring every year to fill up our "Show-off" designated slot. While other classes use one table to display their goods, I require three.

And everything old is new once more, and as Providence decrees, "What has been done, will be done (or worn) again." Only this time around, those bell-bottom pants are made of spandex that snuggles like a second skin around calves and thighs. The hula hoop craze of the 50s and '60s has now morphed into serious competition in the Olympic Games, not to mention those heavy-duty exercise hoops advertised to whirl away unwanted pounds.

Did you know that hoops can be traced back to before Bible times? Ancient drawings on Egyptian pillars depict man's fascination with the rings even then. As King Solomon once said, "There is nothing new under the sun." And I contend that the "nothing" includes man's natural fear of "monsters" — imagined or real — as illustrated in the Old Testament glory-story of David and Goliath.

As the Bible tells us the tale, not one soldier in King Saul's army stepped up to the plate to face the invading Philistines' giant monster, Goliath. No matter the prize, not even one general offered to defend their homeland. Which, in this case, was Solomon's daughter's hand in marriage. Pretty big deal if you ask me.

But when young David — a mere shepherd boy between thirteen and fifteen years old, according to Bible scholars — heard the monster Goliath's taunts, he immediately sought King Saul to volunteer his service as a giant slayer.

The only difference between David and Saul's mighty army of scaredy cats was that David knew his God. He didn't just know *about* him, but he'd taken the time to develop a personal relationship with the God of Abraham, Isaac, and Jacob.

As the story goes, this stub of a faith-filled boy took his staff in his hand, chose five smooth stones from the stream, put them in the pouch of his shepherds pouch, and with his sling in his hand approached the Philistine without fear. What David said and did next in facing the enemy back then is today our own key to victory in spiritual warfare.

He *shouted* — neither talked nor suggested some sort of negotiation meeting — He roared like a lion, "You come against me with a sword (mockery) and spear (intimidation) and javelin (fear), but I come against you in the Name of the Lord Almighty, the God of the Armies of Israel, whom you have defied!"

And therein lies the key to our victory over demonic Goliaths today, providing us the perfect object lesson in how we are to do battle over our kids with the Word of God. But don't just read it.

Don't just pray.

Say it!

Roar it!

Release God's all-powerful promises and the authority of those promises into your home's atmosphere. For the "monsters" we face today are way more dangerous to our families than one giant. They are demons sent by Satan himself to kill, steal, and destroy.

David knew His God. He knew His Word. And he used God's Word to win the battle against the forces of Hell that day. He wasn't afraid of scary monsters hiding in the dark, under his bed, behind closed doors whispering lies, crouched and ready to spring. All begging the question: Why do our little ones, almost universally, think about monsters and, or angels? Why do children wake up at night screaming because some scary monster is chasing them? Why do they creep to peek around corners to make sure a beast isn't waiting for them. Why are they afraid of the dark?

The fear of darkness, especially being alone in the dark, is said to be one of the biggest terrors kids experience. Yet the irony for me today is that when my three little grandnephews come to visit, invariably they beg-beg-beg: "Barry! Donna! Can we play Monsters?" Which is just a scarier version of the traditional Hide-and-Seek Game, but played in the dark with flashlights.

First, we flip off all the house lights. The dinosaur "monsters" (usually my husband and yours-truly) count loudly to thirty, then roar in our nastiest, thunderous, gross voices, "Fe—Fi—Fo—Fum! I smell the blood of an Englishman!" Then comes the yelps of discovery as we all run, scream, and giggle, whether we are the hunted or the hunters.

So, why do kids love to feel . . . terrified? Is it part of an inborn defense mechanism to ward off their genuine fear of the dark? Of sounds they hear in the night. Or monsters they see on the TV ("tell a vision") screen?

But while my brother and sisters and I hid behind our bedroom pillows to sneak-peek at the likes of Dracula, Frankenstein, and the original Mummy, today's kids are dealing with a very real wickedness, much more sinister than that of what they might see on the silver screen. Evil is spinning around and around their worlds, like a perpetual hula hoop of horror, to rob our children of their innocence. To entrap them in the "Dark Side:" Ouija boards, tarot cards, crystals, astrology, seances, levitations and even child trafficking . . .

On the opposite end of this scary spectrum, why can little ones see angels while the rest of us view only an empty corner of the room? Why do they dream of heavenly beings, sometimes even have conversations with them, while we grownups question the reality of what they're seeing or talking about.

Such is the case with Akiane Kramarik, a young self-taught artist who says Jesus spoke to her when she was four years old, encouraging her to draw and paint her visions. The remarkable thing, other than her astonishing colossal portraits of Jesus, is that her parents were atheists! Never went near a church. Never talked about religion. Never even mentioned God in passing.

Another child, Colton Burpo, also four at the time, claims he sat on Jesus' lap. After his appendix burst and undergoing two emergency surgeries, Colton was hanging on by a thread. But while his parents watched his operation procedure from the viewing room, he was up in Heaven meeting his grandfather he never knew. And his sister! The remarkable thing is that Colton's parents, Todd and Sonya, had never told Colton about his miscarried older sister.

"She looked familiar," Colton said, "and she started giving me hugs and told me she was glad to have someone from her family up there. She doesn't have a name though because you never gave her one," he told his mommy and daddy. "But, it's okay. She can't wait to meet you in Heaven. Then you can give her a name!"

Now comes the most fantastic part of both children's stories. Colton's parents kept trying to get him to describe what Jesus looked like after he visited Heaven, showing him picture after picture of various artists' renditions painted over hundreds of years: "No, that's not him . . . not him, either . . . Jesus doesn't look like any of these pictures!" Colton would always respond.

They forgot about their search until one day, seven years later, Colton saw Akiane's *Prince of Peace* portrait of Jesus on TV. He jumped up, excited and pointing: "Dad, that one's right! There he is! That's Jesus!"

Both of these true stories of twenty-first-century children beg the question: could it be that because kids are naturally much closer to Heaven than adults, they can easily experience the supernatural? Only a few years out of the womb, still pure and innocent, perhaps little ones can see into the realm of the heavens. At the same time, we adults have long passed through the portal of innocence to lose our spiritual vision.

I share all this with you to reflect upon the mysteries pondered by mankind since Adam and Eve walked in the Garden with their God before falling for Satan's deceit. Though trends may come and go, Biblical Monsters (demons) are very real, sent to steal, kill, and destroy our children. Our values. Our nation.

So, let's teach ourselves and our kids how to fight back with the authority of David, using the Word of God as our slingshot. Perhaps you even want to buy them a hula hoop, too. You never know when this old-but-new fad might disappear from the sales racks again.

> *So put on God's armor now! Then when the evil day comes,*
> *you will be able to resist the enemy's attacks;*
> *and after fighting to the end, you will still hold your ground.*

Ephesians 3: 16 (GNT)

Hug The Cross

The TV blasts its nightly slop of gruesome potpourri,
While supermarket tabloids ooze their fleeting vanity;
Crass headlines scream unending rage in days of chronic loss,
Lewd voices, swimming in my head, drive me to hug The Cross:

Murder, incest, rape, and theft, adultery, poverty,
Earthquakes, floods and genocide, wars, conspiracy,
Kidnapped, skyjacked, suicide bombs, all butchers for their cause,
Incapacitating heartache compelling me to hug The Cross.

As future heirs are slaughtered before ever drawing breath,
Abortion tolls the bell of doom that quickly speeds their death;
Brash activists unite to charge our pillars. All seems lost.
And still, I grip the splintered wood, once more to hug The Cross.

Dictators rise to lure their prey with promises of wealth,
Depraved fanatics, wicked men, of vile cunning stealth,
Their trophies crowning tombstones in the wake of holocaust.
Victims, splayed on blood-soaked timber, died to hug The Cross.

Depression crouches at my door; Despair's a step away.
Old weariness sits on my shoulders, heavy in the fray.
Cruel winds threaten my balance as they slash, and crush, and toss;
Stripped naked, I hold steadfast to the beam and hug The Cross

Fighting ego — brooding cauldron of conceit and selfish pride.
Where bitterness extends its fangs when devils cast their lies;
Temptation preens to hide its guilt in spotlights of applause.
Broken now — my shame to hide — I weep and hug The Cross

Joining Daniel in the Lion's Den, and Paul thrown into prison,
In confidence my soul yet sings, for glorious Hope has risen,
Laying bare this humble Tree-Of-Life, for all who count the cost
To embrace it as a lover. May we live to hug The Cross.

Peanut Butter and Jelly

"Let your life lightly dance on the edges of time like dew on the tip of a leaf"
Rabindranath Tagore

It was late spring, and the lot still stood empty. "They should be here by now," my husband yelled over his shoulder, a ring of concern in his voice. I grinned, shaking my head in amusement as we maneuvered our bicycles around the sharp right turn to tackle the uphill slope in front of us. Every day, for the past week now, I had heard this same lament.

Precisely who "they" were did not really matter to Barry. All he knew was the anonymous traveling camper home was not in its designated place as it had been for the past five years we'd been bicycling this particular route. It had usually rolled in by May to comfortably nestle next to the white ranch-style house set back off the road amidst adjoining corn fields.

Welcome to my world, or I should say Barry's world. Like most married couples, my husband and I are as different as peanut butter and jelly. He's the peanut butter, of course. I'm the jelly. For while I'm pedaling along drinking in the fresh fragrance of newly popped lilacs, marveling at the ruffling white blossoms of pear trees, or lifting my head to smile at the squawking argument of a pair of Canadian geese winging against a blazing blue sky, Barry is just waiting for this ride to be over.

And in his waiting, he believes it's his preordained mission in life to worry about other people's unfinished chores: "Those people better get that garbage can lid picked up from their lawn. It's been three days now, and the grass underneath will die."

He actually told the couple that owned that particular house of his concern when we saw them getting into their car that day. Fortunately, our new neighbors just laughed at him. The next day, the lid was gone.

"I cannot believe the way they're pouring that driveway!" he'd lamented yesterday as we pedaled by yet another new house going up. "And did you see how high that final porch step is from the ground? Someone's going to break their neck!" No, I hadn't noticed, but I assured him they, no doubt, had a solution to both possible hazards.

I don't know why Barry notices the things he does, or why he worries about them. Why, instead of enjoying our moment in the sunshine, he chooses to worry about getting home to mow the lawn. What I do know is that I adore this crazy man God has blessed me with.

I'd almost chickened out of marrying him in another lifetime. That was when he'd driven me home — 150 miles away from where we were teaching at the time — the day of my wedding shower to announce to my frazzled mother that I was canceling the wedding.

That's right! She'd worked hard all the previous week to prepare the food, not to mention that she had to call all the invited guests — just two hours before the scheduled party! — to inform them that her oldest daughter was not tying the knot, after all.

I was so afraid of making a mistake. How could I know that Barry was the "one?" How could I be sure it would last? That I'd be happy? I'd been through so much pain and trauma due to my parent's divorce. And when I looked around, it seemed I saw very few happily married couples. And then there was the sexual abuse I'd suffered from my grandfather.

Yet, for reasons I'll never understand, Barry stuck by me, assuring me he knew it would work. That *we* would work. Although neither of us were professing Jesus-Lovers (Christians) at the time, Barry's aunt persuaded us that very day to see her pastor for counseling. He turned out to be a Godsend, empathetic and wise.

After interviewing us separately, he calmly told Barry, "What you are dealing with here, Young Man, is a highly emotional, sensitive young lady. You will have to be extremely gentle and understanding in your relationship with her."

In other words, I was a basket case.

Today, like everything else in our 21st Century upside-down, inside-out world, the experts have a special word to describe my ditzy personality. "Decidophobia," according to those in the know, is usually caused by "a traumatic event that is emotionally very painful."

Looking back today, I can see that I fit that description pretty well. My home life wasn't exactly one I wanted to emulate. But after long, tearful, heartfelt conversations, no doubt with a sigh of relief and crossing his fingers, Barry once again slid my exquisite diamond engagement ring back on the third finger of my left hand where it belonged.

Eventually, we addressed envelopes together to send out a second round of wedding invitations, again inviting friends and family to share in our *new* special day with the unspoken promise that the bride would follow through this time.

I'm sorry to say my cancelled bridal shower never saw the light of a new day. This probably delighted our invited guests because they already had the perfect gift, still wrapped and waiting to be recycled. All they had to do was switch out the cards, swapping the shower card for a happy wedding day greeting.

I was ready to take the plunge to find my "happily ever after." Even so, on the sparkling snowy morning of my wedding day, I awoke to kneel at my bedside with a frantic plea to a God I hoped existed: "If you don't want me to do this, please stop it somehow!"

And my good-good Heavenly Father gently pushed me down the aisle.

Today, I can say marrying Barry was the second-best decision I have ever made. The first was the day three years later when my sweetie and I asked Jesus Christ to be the "Bread of Life" to hold our peanut butter and jelly marriage together. Don't get me wrong. We both still think the other is weird on occasion. Okay, more often than not. But we also deeply love and respect each other, more so every minute, every day, and every passing year.

We decided long ago that peanut butter and jelly are what every kid knows is a yummy combination. While peanut butter (Barry) is a little too dry by itself, it needs a spoonful of jelly (yours truly) to sweeten it up a bit. To add a fruity zing to its sticky, dry, heavy texture.

Jelly, on the other hand, needs the stabilizing influence of the peanut butter, or it tends to slip and slide all over the place. But together, the two bond perfectly into one yummy sandwich—just like Barry and me—in an unbeatable combination.

And now these three remain: faith, hope and love.
But the greatest of these is love.

I Corinthians 13:13 (NIV)

Making Our Bed Together

From the moment we get up
to make our bed together,
through all the in-between
tick-tocks of the clock:

Reading Words of Life,
praying hand-in-hand,
two hands clasped as one
in sunshine, sleet, and snow.

Laughing at each other,
crying tears of agony,
talking through problems,
cheering each other on.

Swallowing words of hurt,
bellowing irritations,
choosing to see the good
within the safety of your hug.

Until we pull the covers back,
drifting off to sleep,
rising another day
to make our bed together.

The Lame Man Who Taught Me How to Dance

By Sharon James

"Those who were seen dancing were thought to be insane by those who could not hear the music."
Friedrich Nietzsche

One summer, my husband and I escaped to the captivating island of Bermuda, where the water is crystalline blue and the air wafts of blooming hibiscus. The vacation was complete with long romantic walks on white sandy beaches, splashing waves on limestone rock jetties, and discoveries of secluded ocean-carved caves. At night, a choir of tiny green Bermuda tree frogs sang romantic cadences just for us.

I'll never forget one evening when Steve and I went on a dining adventure to a five-star restaurant filled with men and women dressed in their finest evening apparel. The semicircular dining room was lined with glass, which overlooked the Atlantic Ocean and allowed the flaming orange-red of the setting sun to be our backdrop.

In one corner of the dining area, a four-person ensemble filled the room with fluid sounds of music from the 40's and 50's. Steve and I had taken a few ballroom dance lessons, and he wanted us to see if we could remember the steps. "Come on, Sharon," he urged. "Let's go take a spin on the dance floor and see if we can still do the Foxtrot."

"Nobody else is out there," I replied. "I don't want to be the only one on the floor with everyone staring at me. Besides, it's been a long time since we've danced, and I don't remember all the steps." I saw the disappointment rise in his eyes so quickly added, " How about if we wait until other people fill the open spaces? Then I'll go."

I've read that the Foxtrot was the most significant development in ballroom dancing. According to history books, the beginning of the 20th century in America gave birth to this splendid and one-of-a-kind fun dance named after the vaudeville actor Harry Fox.

According to legend, he could not find a female dancer capable of performing the more difficult two-step, so he added "stagger steps" (two trots) to create today's Foxtrot rhythm of "slow-slow-quick-quick." The dance premiered in 1914, quickly catching the eye of the talented husband-wife team duo Vernon and Irene Castle, who lent the dance the signature grace and style we see today.

Well, I certainly was no Irene Castle, nor was my hubby even close to capturing the grace of her husband Vernon, but we'd had a ball trying to learn this fun dance.

After what must have seemed unbearably long to my impatient husband, the first couple finally approached the floor. As they began, they looked like professional dancers, moving around the smooth surface in a symbiotic fluid motion of grace. This did not encourage me at all but strengthened my resolve to stay glued to my comfy seat.

Then Couple Number 1 was joined by Couple Number 2, whose steps weren't quite as perfect. "Okay," I said, standing up from my chair, "Now I'll go. But let's go in the back corner behind that Ficus Tree where nobody can see us, okay?"

So off we trotted (no pun intended) to our little spot on the shiny parquet dance floor to try to replicate the 1-2-3-4's of the Foxtrot. After a few moments, however, I noticed a fourth couple approaching. They entered the floor with confidence — no hesitation — no timidity. But, this twosome was extraordinary: the man was in a wheelchair.

He was a middle-aged, slightly balding, large-framed guy with a neatly trimmed beard. On his left hand, he wore a white glove. Although I guessed it had nothing to do with his admiration for Michael Jackson, it was most likely to cover a skin disease.

Although he and his wife were dressed to the hilt in stunning evening wear, it was their radiant smiles that reflected the most beautiful part of their approach. Their love for each other lit up the room.

As the band played a peppy beat, the wife held her love's healthy right hand and danced back and forth with him. He never did rise from the wheelchair that had become his legs, but they didn't seem to care. They came together and separated like expert dancers. He spun her around, and she stooped to conform to his seated position.

Lovingly, like a little fairy child, she danced around his chair while his laughter became the fifth instrument in this small orchestra. Even though his feet did not move from their metal resting place, his shoulders swayed in perfect time, and his eyes danced with hers.

My heart was so moved by this love story unfolding before my eyes that I had to turn my head and bury my face on Steve's shoulder so no one would see the tears streaming down my cheeks. When I looked up, I beheld a room full of tears as linen napkins dabbed tearful eyes. Even the band members seemed transfixed by this portrait of love and devotion.

Then, the music slowed to a lazy romantic melody, and the man's wife pulled up a chair beside her love's but faced in the opposite direction. Together, their upper bodies formed the dancer's frame with one arm extended and the other snuggling close.

Now, cheek-to-cheek, they swayed to the piano man's melody. At one point, they both closed their eyes as if remembering, dreaming of an earlier time when his chair did not restrain their hunger to dance with each other.

After watching this incredible display of love and courage, I realized that my inhibitions of not wanting others to watch me because my steps may not be perfect were petty.

God spoke to my heart: "Sharon, I want you to notice who moved this crowd to tears."

"It wasn't the first couple, with their flawless steps, nor was it this last couple, who had no steps at all. But their display of devotion and affection, not practiced perfection, stirred the peoples' hearts."

It's like he was saying if you do what I've called you to do, I will do it for you just as his wife did for him. It's not perfect steps, Sharon, that will change the world. It's the courage to take the first step in the dance of obedience to me.

I realized then my steps would always be flawed on a dance floor or, more importantly, in life. But our Heavenly Father doesn't expect our steps to be perfect. What he does expect is that we listen for His voice, those small nudges that seem to come out of nowhere, that we lean into obedience, and that we take that first step of faith.

The tuxedoed man in that wheelchair never even moved his feet, I thought, but his wife led him in the steps. And we must remember that the Lord will do this for us, too.

That night, on Bermuda's beautiful shores, the Lord sent me a lame man to teach me how to dance with Him, the Creator of the Universe. I don't have to worry about being "good enough." I simply need to walk in tandem with Jesus, or in this case, dance to His lead, and He will lead me by still waters to find the pathway he wants to take me next.

The heart of a man plans his way, but the Lord established his steps.

Proverbs 16:9 (ESV)

Perfect
Timing

by Dawn Damon

"In life, as in dance, grace glides on blistered feet."
Alice Abrams

The captain's voice blared through the crackling speakers delivering the unwelcome announcement no airline passenger wants to hear. I covered my ears to muffle the piercing sound, but I heard him loud and clear, "Ladies and Gentlemen, this is your captain. Storm clouds loom ahead, and we expect to encounter some turbulence. For your safety, please remain in your seats and buckle your seatbelts. Flight attendants, please take your seats."

Securing my seatbelt with an extra tug, I downed the last remnants of my diet coke and braced for the impending tempest. In mere moments, our aircraft plunged into the heart of the dark clouds, jolting violently through the storm-laden sky.

It wasn't the first time I'd experienced turbulence; I'm a seasoned traveler, so I wasn't completely freaked out, but I was agitated. What if this storm makes me late? I hope we can land. The dinner event tonight is crucial. I don't want to miss it.

I was flying clear across the country to attend an industry conference. I was especially looking forward to the opening group dinner. Many vital connections occur at these networking dinners. It was a definite highlight, and I had prepared my new business cards and flyers, ready to meet new friends and make strategic contacts.

Crack!

Thud!

The violent clatter jerked my mind back to the present. The aircraft rattled with force as we navigated the tumultuous skies. Once again, the captain's voice filled the cabin: "Ladies and Gentlemen, we must circle the airport. Due to strong winds, the tower has instructed us not to land. We hope to touch down in 30-40 minutes."

Urgh! Delayed. As my hopes for an on-time arrival dwindled, my agitation only intensified. I tried to muster some encouragement. *Perhaps I can still make the end of the dinner if the pilot sets this bird down in the next half-hour.*

He did.

Jubilant cheers erupted among the passengers as the plane wobbled to a safe landing. Despite the ticking clock, I shared in their elation. Based on my calculations, I could still make the evening events.

Several minutes passed until I finally scrambled off the plane and sprinted with blistered feet to the baggage claim area. In my haste, I devised a new strategy. I took my phone and ordered an Uber driver. My plan seemed logical: get to baggage claim, grab my suitcase, dash out the airport door, and seamlessly lilt into the waiting Uber. Perfect. Or so I thought.

Once more, however, my plan was thwarted as I listened to yet another un-welcome announcement. Storm-induced chaos had thrown synchronized plane schedules into disarray, causing an unforeseen logjam and further delays in baggage retrieval.

"Oh no! Another delay," I grumbled in frustration. Attending the opening dinner seemed increasingly unlikely. My irritation peaked as I thought about how meticulously I had planned everything, only for this annoying disruption to happen. My grievances were abruptly halted by the ringing of my phone. It was my Uber driver, urgently stating, "If you don't come now, I'll have to leave. The airport won't let me wait." Overwhelmed, I conceded defeat, agonizing over the realization that I would not be present for dinner. "Just go," I sighed.

I paced the crowded baggage claim area, empathizing with other weary travelers running thin on grace. Forty-five minutes later, my suitcase tumbled out of the conveyor belt. I hoisted it up on its wheels, and trudged out the door. By now, my Uber driver was long gone, and so was my patience. Still, I found the grit to make my way to the rear of the transportation queue and claim the next available taxicab. After another 15 minutes, the yellow taxi pulled up for me. I slumped into the backseat, discouraged, tired, and out of grace. At long last, I was headed down the highway, just in time for the 5:00 o'clock rush hour.

"Sorry, ma'am," said Samuel, the driver. "This rush hour will slow us down."

"Of course it will," I snarked. "Everything has been late today, Samuel. My perfectly constructed plans have completely bombed. Nothing has worked out the way I had hoped. All I can say is, I give up."

"Well, Ma'am, sometimes that's what God wants us to do. Surrender. Give our plans over to him. There's no sense in fighting what we can't control, right? In times like these, trust God and His perfect timing."

Samuel's kind words encouraged my heart as he spoke for several miles. "Of course, you're right," I managed to respond.

And then, in the hushed confines of the long taxi ride, with fatigue and disappointment settling in, I repented of my irritation. "God, forgive me for allowing these circumstances to steal my joy. I surrender my frustration and choose to trust you. Your timing is perfect, and your plans surpass mine. Thank you for sending Samuel to remind me that your grace is more than enough. I am truly grateful."

Upon reaching the conference hotel, a sense of renewal washed over me. The vibrant conversation with Samuel had breathed life into my weary spirit, igniting a fresh sense of purpose. In truth, I had been carrying a weighty burden and grappling with feeling overwhelmed for quite some time. Could it be that this divine encounter with Samuel was orchestrated by God to minister to my weary heart? Was this God's timing all along?

The lobby was nearly vacant when I rolled into the hotel conference center. As expected, the festive events for the evening were over. I had missed out. Delays ruined my plans. But I was not defeated. God's plan had prevailed for me, and I was convinced something special was about to unfold.

Seizing a quiet moment to reflect, I grabbed a firelit restaurant table for a bite to eat, reassuring myself that tomorrow held the promise of a great day, when unexpectedly I noticed two familiar women waving with welcoming smiles. While I hadn't met them in person, I recognized them as the conference hosts. They beckoned me over. "Join us! You must be here for the conference. We'd love to meet you."

Over the next two hours, I had the most enjoyable and memorable encounter. We delved into deep and meaningful discussions, laying the foundation for a precious friendship that endures to this day. God had choreographed the perfect evening, skillfully weaving together a master plan, unfolding—not in mine—but in his impeccable timing.

"Lord, thank you for ordering my steps, and my stops," I whispered. And with that, I smiled as God's grace filled my heart.

Trust in the LORD with all your heart, and do not lean on your own understanding. In all your ways acknowledge him, and he will make straight your paths.

Proverbs 3:5-6 (ESV)

Alarm Clock Negotiations

The alarm clock is screaming, now I have a choice,
To bounce from my bed or to kill its shrill voice.
Return to the comfy and cozy of slumber,
Or rise-up-and-shine to embrace the day's wonder.

I hear the birds chirping, "Get up and get dressed!"
My pillow objects, whispering, *"You need your rest!"*
Recalling the sleep-ins of sweet auld-langsyne,
The sandman still lulls me, seducing my mind:

Just ten-minutes more in this sweet La-La-Land,
Before groggy-groping to reach the nightstand,
Where sanity beckons from daybreak's threshold:
You're blessed beyond measure if truth would be told.

I crawl from my hideout to shake off the groggy,
To stretch out the drowsy, and clear out the froggy,
To wiggle my tickle — adjust — realign . . .
My attitude's gratitude . . . "Hello, Sunshine!"

Groovers, Movers, And Rollers

by Amber Weigand-Buckley

*Let them praise His name with dancing
and make music to Him with timbrel and harp.
Psalm 149:3 (NIV)*

I'll never forget the lady who taught me to dance like no one is watching. Her name was Downtown Julie Brown, and she hosted Club MTV—a show my conservative parents didn't know I could access through our bedroom cable box. When Julie introduced hits like "Never Gonna Give You Up," "Beat It," or "Walking on Sunshine," after school, my little sister Lorrie and I sprang into action. Homework forgotten, curtains drawn, bedroom transformed—we covertly choreographed and practiced our smooth moves for hours. I mastered the "Roger Rabbit," "Running Man," and "Cabbage Patch" as Lorrie kept pace.

We may not have had an actual dance floor, but flashing the lights created a makeshift disco ambiance. Between Julie's infectious energy and our overflowing enthusiasm, our after-school dance sessions equipped me with moves for some of the most memorable nights of my teenage life. While my parents thought I was studying, I secretly learned to dance like no one was watching from the best teacher around.

True worship reflects God's worthiness, not our performance. I can't remember where I heard this idea, but the words still stick in my spirit—they are an example of the pure joy of dance that can't be contained. Because of who He is, not about how good we were able to break it down on the dance floor or the spotlight being on us.

Our private dance parties became sacred spaces to connect with God through joyful movement and praise, not bound by expectations. Whenever I had the opportunity to bust a move at a high school dance on the weekend, my friend Tabby readily offered to "host me for sleepovers." This provided the perfect cover story for my parents who believed that any music-influenced movement that lifted your feet from the floor led you — feet first — into the fire and brimstone.

Tabby and I also boldly crashed the local senior center's monthly polka night dances, where sweet elderly folks amusedly twirled us around the floor. However, nothing compared to the alternate universe awaiting each week at Christian Skate Night.

Getting Our Holy Rollers On

Clouds of the stale leather floated up as Tabby and I added another layer of blister protection to our stacked socks and laced up the well-scuffed and creased rentals, wheels soon humming atop the polished hardwood. The DJ seamlessly blended beloved upbeat Christian hits with danceable beats as the lights lowered and the mirror balls scattered stars everywhere. Jamming along to Petra and Whiteheart classics, we belted out every word at the top of our lungs while getting our groove on. Spinning and bopping counter-clockwise during the nightly "all skate" under the splash of colors felt almost spiritual as we bonded with friends bathed in light and motion.

Being an awkwardly tall 5'11" girl, I flew solo when Couples' Skates played since intimidated boys didn't often approach me. But I'd proudly bop around the floor, anyway, lip-syncing along. More than just chaotic exercise, the convergence of music, wheels, and movement transported me to someplace magical. The rhythm vibrating from the floor through my wheels, the kinship of community, the resonance deep in my soul for that glorious window in time, I tapped into the flow of a divinely-inspired dance.

I'm pretty sure my devout parents would've done a double take if they had witnessed their once-innocent daughter "popping and locking" under the glittering disco lights to "Jesus Freak." But we weren't challenging our faith — we were just finding new ways to celebrate it.

Our rebellion was harmless, driven by a desire to express ourselves and embrace the rhythm in our veins.

We weren't breaking commandments, just "breaking it down" on the dance floor. Secret dance parties and dominating Christian Skate Night were tame in the grand scheme of teenage rebellion. (My pierced ears from a senior trip to Texas probably shocked them more!)

From the infectious beats of Petra's "Beat the System" to the pop rhythms of Amy Grant's "Baby-Baby," our rebellion had a beat you could roll to.

The humor lies in the fact that rebellious as I thought I was, I was just a teenager finding joy in dancing. Who can blame me? Dancing is a celebration of life, a universal language connecting people. A chance to let go, express, and connect with something greater.

Tabby and I discovered profound spiritual connection and expression in that mix of 80's Christian pop, rock, and dance melodies. As King David reflected, there is a "time for everything under heaven" (Ecclesiastes 3:4), including letting joy spill out through movement and music.

Contemporary Christian singer Carman captured that freeing call to expression in his song "Revival in the Land" with the lyrics: "We're a revelation generation with fire in our bones!" For us, those dance floors served as our sanctuaries where everyone joyfully sang the words straight from their hearts and moved however the Spirit spontaneously led in that moment. We were just answering the call deep inside to join the praise revolution.

"Dance is the hidden language of the soul," choreographer Martha Graham observed. Reflecting years later, I recognize a deeper significance in what felt like silly, harmless fun. Through Dance's rhythms, steps, and creative self-expression, we tapped into our true essence in ways beyond ordinary words. Dance took us to profound places where we could simply exist in the moment, connect to others' spirits, and bask in the joy of being alive.

Now in my 50s, I still feel that irrepressible urge to move when certain melodies stir my spirit. My dance floor today may look more like the Walmart frozen food aisle, but I invariably find myself shuffling and twirling to the piped-in hits. The music instantly transports me through a time portal back to that transcendent well of celebration and praise that dance opens up.

Where I used to secretly dance barefoot in my bedroom "if you want to" like David, now I boldly invite others to join in throughout my days. As the psalmist proclaimed, "Let them praise His name with dancing!" (Psalm 149:3). I celebrate God's presence and divine rhythm pulsing through all of life's ordinary moments and locations. For me, every impromptu step, every little sway or swivel still naturally harmonizes movement with that transcendent mystery and glory, regardless of age, location, audience, or ability.

Today I encourage you to also listen when the melody's irresistible call rises within. Release worry over others' eyes and put on your dancing shoes. Or wheels if your spirit moves you. Discover your dance, even with two left feet, to join in the eternal dance of life.

May our vision never be clouded by our self-imposed limitations or false self-judgment. Open your arms to receive each moment's invitation to Joy. Listen as your soul whispers, calling you to freely unite with the music. May your dance floor become a sanctuary, celebration, and connection to the Divine presence, shaking things up and around you. Are you ready? The time for your holy dance revolution awaits!

And David danced before the Lord with all his might,

2 Samuel 6:14a (NLT)

I Am Dance

I rise up
on wings of eagles,
—strong, majestic—
flirting with undercurrents
begging me to soar. Beguiling,
the music captures me, and I take flight,
no longer belonging to this earth,
but to eternity, past and future,
yet always in the ever-present
moment as wave upon wave
of magic engulfs me
into a new birth
of movement:
I am Dance!

Slow Dancing With The King

"I waltzed with the Lord of the Dance just moments ago, where I found it was
okay to dance inside an empty tomb."
Donna Arlynn Frisinger

Some moments in a lifetime are so unforgettable that you can recall
them at will, and every smile, touch, and tear washes over your soul as
if it had just happened. The day I slow-danced with Jesus both broke
my heart and healed it, all at the same time.

My mother was not having a good day. If there is such a thing as a
good day in the Alzheimer's unit of a nursing home, it was when I
could make eye contact with her to catch a glimpse of my old playmate
peek-a-booing from behind her present-day mask of confusion and
fear. When I could hear the lilt of her laughter. See her eyes light up
when I stepped into her room to visit: "Oh, Donna! I'm so glad you're
here."

But that morning, I couldn't even get her to look at me — this woman
who'd belly-laughed so hard with me over the years we'd end up in tears.
Or wetting our pants. This sister-in-Christ, who'd danced winsome waltzes
with The King until she could no longer stand on her own feet. Did she

dance with Him still, I wondered, somewhere inside that joyless, forbidden world I couldn't penetrate?

"Life Care Center."

That's what they call it.

I found that title dismally inappropriate. How anyone could call my mother's existence *"Life"* — a daily hibernating on a squat flowered couch, slumped over like a propped-up Humpty-Dumpty — was beyond my understanding.

Once, years ago, I'd promised her she'd never end up in such a place. Back then, Mom had been working as a nurse's aide in the same nursing home where I now found myself. Changing sheets, wiping raw behinds, lifting crippled bodies onto the same squat flowered couches. She'd been their special angel: "Arlene, hold my hand . . . Sing me a song . . . Tell me a story . . ."

That particular afternoon, we had just finished our weekly walk in the Tippecanoe State Park. As we'd hunkered down atop a sun-bleached picnic table to munch on our peanut butter and jelly sandwiches, the autumn leaves rained over us in splashes of M&M's confetti. I knew then, I would hide that moment in my soul forever.

She giggled like a schoolgirl, licking grape jelly from her fingers while swiping at a crimson maple leaf stuck upright in her hair. I thought she looked like an Indian Princess, as well she might have been. Mom traced some of her ancestors back to the reservations that dotted the Oklahoma plains in the early 1900s.

"They just want to go home," she was saying of her patients at the nursing home, "and they don't understand why they can't. Some of them have no one who comes to visit them. It's heartbreaking, Donna. I don't ever want to end up in that place."

"Don't worry, Mom, I'll never let you go into a nursing home."

One should be more careful about what pops out of our mouths, like the surprise puppet inside an old-fashioned Jack-in-the-Box that springs up at the song's end. We never know when our words will later bushwhack us with remembrance and regret. But how could I have possibly known that day in the woods of the stalking, sinister monster that would sneak into our lives to steal my mother away?

As I'd attempted to visit with her this morning, a new roommate's over-sized TV boomed a senseless soap opera so loud that it hurt my ears. Trying to find someone to fix the problem had proven futile. "Well, that lady is almost deaf, you know."

Even so, Mom seemed unresponsive as I bent to gently kiss her brow before murmuring my wistful benediction as I prepared to leave. "I love you so much, Mommy. Go on home to Jesus. It's Okay."

Back home now, in my living room, I flipped the switch to the stereo and the tranquil strains from a favorite praise-and-worship CD filled the air. I collapsed to the floor, clutching at my stomach, rocking back and forth, sobbing. I desperately wanted to vomit out the intense torture that twisted in my gut. "Jesus," I pleaded, "please, take her home today."

Immediately, I sensed a presence. An electrifying, pulsating energy. Within the fragmented burst of light streaming through my picture window's half-open vertical blinds, I saw Jesus extending his hand to me in open invitation.

Fragile, trembling, and spellbound, I rose to step into His arms.

Was this really happening?

We swayed like young lovers, barely moving our feet, as a violin solo inter-twined with heavenly harmony from an unseen orchestra in three-quarter time: *"Jesus . . . Jesus . . . Jesus . . . There's just something about that name . . . "*

Goosebumps tingled up my spine and down my arms when I felt his warm hand resting against the small of my back. Fresh tears flowed from a buried reservoir that kept filling up and emptying again. Would this agony of spirit ever stop? Get any easier to bear? I remembered Mom had once told me that she couldn't cry anymore. That her tear ducts had all dried up. Emptied out over a lifetime of hurt, struggle, and shattered expectations.

But she'd been wrong.

In the world of Alzheimer's, they call it "Sundown Syndrome." My step-dad Don would call around 7:00 p.m. every night, his voice cracked and crusty with grief. By this time of day, his ability to cope had stretched to the breaking point. "Donna, your mother needs to talk to you."

Mom's broken, sniffling voice would then proceed to cut yet another wedge into my already hemorrhaging heart when he'd hand her the phone: "Donna...?"

"What's wrong, Mommy? Do you need me to come over?"

"Oh, Honey, would you?"

She'd be waiting for me when I pulled into the driveway. As we held each other, our tears mingled in an excruciating embrace, arms wrapped so tightly around each other that our spirits intertwined to drown in a murky well of no return. "I'm sooo scared," she'd whimper.

"I know, Mommy."

And I did know. Because I was scared, too. For her. For me. For what lay ahead. But mostly for realizing I was totally helpless to stop this "Life Thief." And that knowing gnawed at me even now, slow-dancing with my King in this sacred moment inside my own living room. I rested my head against His bosom, and I heard the *thud-thud* of His heartbeat. Or was it mine?

Initially, Mom, not unlike her previous patients, had wanted nothing more than to go home. That was in the early days after Don had dropped her off at the nursing home. After he'd limped away down a too-long hallway on crippled knees, rivers of self-reproach and remorse cut gullies down his sunken, weathered cheekbones.

This was the love of his life he was leaving behind. His camping buddy of the past twenty-five years. His "let's go for a ride" sidekick loved cuddling with him on the swing in their backyard, watching the sun kiss the corn-fields goodnight. His partner-in-crime when they'd jump up and head to McDonalds for their favorite caramel sundaes.

Heartache.

We all live with it.

Deal with it in different ways.

This is not Heaven, after all.

Some of us try to ignore this boogeyman called Grief by keeping busy. Not thinking about it. If we can just keep juggling all the balls without dropping them, running on the proverbial treadmill of our own making while maintaining our balance, perhaps we can bypass the heartaches of life. Keep our earbuds in place long enough to block out the inevitable.

Then there are those like me here today, swaying with my welcomed guest in a bittersweet embrace that releases all guilt, even as I held onto the pain in this moment of Thanksgiving. For the living, it represented the tender touches and twitters, the remember-whens, words, and embraces so warm and personal that they are forever nestled inside my heart like a cuddling kitten.

The music ends.

I exhale, at peace now, feeling no condemnation.

Squinting, to find a trace of my eloquent dance partner, I can't focus through my tears, and I wonder: Will I really be able to one day look into the face of God? To dare to probe the eyes of the One who created me? The One who loves me best? And that's when I heard it:

A faint silvery tinkling.

What was that?

Where was it coming from?

I tiptoed toward the sound of the *ding-a-ling,* until . . . *Uh!*

My breath ran away as I gasped in surprise.

Mom had given me the whimsical ceramic figurine for my 21st birthday. Now, safely hidden away on the middle shelf in my dining room hutch, the music box hadn't worked for years. Too many *wound-up-too-tight* turns of the key, compliments of tiny nephew's and niece's curious fingertips.

But now, unbelievably, that long-forgotten treasure — a princess schoolgirl in a pastel blue gown, cradling a bouquet of forget-me-nots to her heart — was slowly twirling to a sweet refrain: *"Somewhere, My Love, there will be songs to sing — although the snow covers the hopes of spring . . ."*

Liquid love streamed down my cheeks. *You'll see her again, Donna. You grieve only for that which you have loved. And what is life, after all, without love? A song with no harmony. A solitary walk in the park. Peanut butter without jelly.*

Brrrrrrring . . . !

I jumped at the ring of the telephone. It was Kelly, my younger sister. "Donna, Mommy just went home to Heaven."

Dropping the phone, I grabbed my keys and dashed to my car to return to the nursing home. But as I drove the maple-lined streets, I noticed their buds about to burst into Spring's new life, and I knew this present sorrow held no power over me. My mother had been dancing in Heaven, even as I'd waltzed with the Lord of the Dance just moments ago, where I found dancing inside an empty tomb was okay.

> *He will wipe every tear from their eyes, and death shall be no more,*
> *neither shall there be Mourning, nor crying, nor pain anymore,*
> *for the former things have passed away.*
> Rev. 2:1 (ESV)

Tribute To Dorothy Arlene

Dear to my heart and my best friend,
Others can never comprehend
Rituals of giggles stored in the bank
Of memories we've shared, nectars we've drank.
Today and tomorrow, forever, you'll be
Heroic, courageous, sweet, gentle and free;
Young at heart always; forever my mother:

An artist, a beauty—unlike no other,
Ready to turn a new page as you've prayed,
Leaning on Jesus, to walk unafraid;
Each day — determined to finish your race,
Never to doubt in His bountiful grace,
Endlessly trusting to gaze on His face.

Pantyhose Ribbon Dance

by Dr. Laura Loveberry

The students of Balboa High School invented the Bunny Hop in San Francisco in the spring of 1952 — *One hop forward, one hop back, hop-hop-hop* ... But for me, one memorable evening, that old dance lived again to hop in an unexpected place.

But I digress. As Julie Andrews so famously sang, "Let's start at the very beginning..."

I strolled into the spacious country club, tilting my head back to better view the rich, luxurious architecture. Wow! This place is fancy-pancy, another lottie-dottie speaking engagement on my current speaking circuit.

Quickly snapping a picture of the crowd in my mind's eye, I looked around at the ladies, all sitting in "proper" posture with their diamond rings flashing and glossy lipstick perfectly lined around their Barbie Doll lips. The decorated tables seemed spoiled somehow with scatterings of Coach purses. I giggle inside. Our guests tonight must have "worked hard enough and long enough."

I say this because of an encounter with the first woman I met that day: "Hey, I like your purse," I said, trying to find common ground. "The design on the handle is really cool."

Rolling her eyes, she answered, "My dear, this is a Coach purse. If you work hard enough and long enough, you too can have a coach purse someday."

Yikes! My eyes popped, and I strained to keep from laughing. Instead, I politely nodded and thanked her for sharing her good fortune with me while biting my lip. Aloofness floats in the air tonight like gossip at a beauty parlor. How will I ever be able to reach these affluent ladies with the true riches found in a relationship with Jesus Christ?

Taking a deep breath, I marched forward.

This brief interlude defines many of my audiences at these fancy clubs I visit when volunteering to speak for "Country Club Ministries." We share the Lord with women where they feel comfortable. This means no church events. No meetings at a religious establishment where unbelievers may feel uncomfortable. Instead, we go to their turf, their clubs, their environment.

The ministry I work with even decorates the tables to encourage smiles. Tonight, I see it obviously delighted our guests to be at this special event. I relax. They relax, right?

Looking forward to this special event planned with just them in mind, our organization rocks at making unique memories for the honored guests. On days like this, I drive hundreds of miles in a tri-state area to carry the Good News of Jesus Christ. We see lives transform.

When I share my God Story, it always starts with describing how I did not fit in with reserved Christians. Most of my audience laughs, but when I was just a ten-year-old girl, some demoralizing kid told me, "Hey Laura, the Bible says the meek will inherit the kingdom of God. You're not meek. You're not going to Heaven."

Since I didn't even own a Bible, I started checking with the grownups in my world: "Do you think I am meek?"

Most of them laughed to eventually say, "No way!" It seemed nobody described me as meek. Their reactions triggered my anxiety complex of not fitting in with the "meek," big-bible-carrying Christians. In my mind, I felt rejected by God. I was too bold for Heaven, so I feared I was going the other direction—Hell. Whoa! The thought traumatized my nights.

Then, as I grew into a flighty teenager, I joined a Christian Club at school. They accepted me and my gregarious personality.

Surprise!

By faith, I believed in Jesus Christ and transformed into a full-fledged follower of the Way, the Truth, and the Life. Now, I understand that Jesus died for my sins to be forgiven. He rose from the dead so I could live in Heaven with him forever.

Now I walked, bouncing a big smile, and never feared the fires of Hell again. But still contemplating my "not-meek-enough" dilemma, I tried to change my personality. This failed. I lived loud and overflowing with energy by nature.

But I started reading my Bible daily and went to a Bible-teaching church where I learned to live by God's principles. My personality matured, and I grew with a God-bent. Oh, I kept my fun-loving ways but dropped the cussing. I no longer rattled off, "Oh my God." Previously, I'd used the slang term repeatedly. And disrespectfully.

In addition, I learned "appropriate behavior," developing a sensitivity to God's Holy Spirit guiding me in my relationships. Finally, I understood God designed me and my flamboyant personality for His glory.

With the banquet meal finished, standing at the podium in front of these elegant women, my mind flutters to ask, "How can I connect?" I say a silent prayer: *Help me, Lord. Empower me, and my words to share your heart.*

I felt things were going pretty well until . . . *Uh-oh!* Something terrible happened. My eyes popped to the size of quarters. My pantyhose released their elasticity. Every thread! Right in the middle of my talk.

My focus is definitely distracted. My "know-how" went haywire. The speech I'd worked so long on to share the hope found in Jesus was wilting, much like my sagging hose.

I mean, seriously, how's a girl supposed to concentrate with her knees pressed hard together while her pantyhose threatens to fall down her legs at any minute?

Sweat beaded on my forehead. Maybe stepping to the side of the podium would help to work my hose back up to my waist?

Nope.

Not a chance. Good grief!

I shuffled back behind the podium, no doubt looking like a Walmart shopper testing new shoes with the connecting plastic tag still attached. Then I stumbled, nearly tripping myself because the crotch of my nylons had now dropped to my knees. Now, I felt them cross the barrier of my hemline. I mean, come on. Not even the Duchess of York herself could focus on delivering a speech under these conditions.

Suppressing the urge to reach down and yank up my silky evaporated waistline, my mind spun, scrambling for a solution. What's Plan B?

Grimacing with embarrassment, I sheepishly announced a leave of absence, hoping my predicament would remain my secret: "Okay, everyone, turn to your neighbor and get acquainted. Tell each other a little bit about yourself. Give them a hug! I — will be right back!"

Executing a shuffling waddle, I made my way to the bathroom door, thankfully located right around the corner. As I bunny-hop forward, properly composed faces crunched, and eyes rolled down to spot my baggy ankles.

More sweat drips.

My eyes twitch as I shuffle out of the suddenly over-heated banquet room. Snickers follow after me.

Finally, stumbling into the restroom, I yank off my failed hosiery, looking for a trash can to pitch them. Then, catching a glimpse of my frazzled face in the mirror, I stop, chuckling, as "Plan B" knocks me up the side of my head. I will entertain these fancy ladies, all right. With a grand re-entrance, they'll never forget.

Now I fist-pump into the air whispering, "Yes!" while smiling boldly at my reflection. Hey, I'm a hot mess, but who cares? I'm on a mission from God, right?

Strutting full stride back into the banquet hall, I hold my bedraggled hosiery high over my head to swirly-loop them in the air like a Gold Medalist Olympic Ribbon Dancer and boisterously announce, "*I'm ba-a-ck!* My pantyhose failed their assignment tonight, but Ladies, nothing will stop my message!"

After the hoots, good-natured laughter, and hollers died down, my no-longer reserved audience leans into my words to listen to what I say. All smiles now, with white teeth flashing, we bond on this night with the gift of silliness and laughter.

Now, I can easily share the truth and freedom I found in a personal relationship with the God of the Universe. I finish up my talk with a bang: "Who wants to put their faith in Jesus Christ right here and now?"

Many make faith decisions for Jesus. Halleluia!

For the other unresponsive gals, seeds are planted into softer soil, the hard-packed clay broken, watered, and fertilized for someone else to harvest. All because I'd chosen to plant the kernel of truth instead of panicking when the walls (hose) came tumbling down.

... for it is God who works in you, to will and to act
in order to fulfill his good purpose.

Philippians 2:13 (NIV)

Hot Baths and Ice Cream

It's the little things I'm grateful for that sets my heart to skipping,
Like racing melting ice cream cones before they start to dripping.

Silly-slurping foaming bubbles at the end of chocolate malts,
Or a hot fudge sundae topping off my spirit's somersaults.

It's the serendipitous pleasures found in friendship's double-dipping,
Metamorphing into lovers, just beginning a courtshipping

With electrifying kisses, holding hands, and saying prayers,
And "I love you's" far more treasured than the gold of millionaires.

It's the melody of laughter that my soul is roundelaying
In the toothless grins of babies, or a toddler's pretend-playing

Of wild pony rides, and "shake-a-butts," or "Let's go to the park!"
Cuddling memories, sipping Chai Tea in the quiet after dark.

It's the soothing sanctuary of the hot bath where I'm soaking:
The submerged, fulfilling revelry, just knowing I'm slow-poking

In this understated wonder-world, evaporating achin'
With just God and me, alone at last, day's cares are all forsaken.

One on One With Mom

By Martha Bolton

"We dance for laughter, we dance for tears, we dance for madness,
we dance for fears, we dance for hopes, we dance for screams,
we are the dancers, we create the dreams."
Albert Einstein

As the youngest of five children, I longed for more one-on-one time with my mother. Not only did she have five of us (and our pets) vying for her attention, but she was also involved with the PTA at our schools, serving as PTA president locally and as the Ways and Means chairwoman for the California State PTA Board. This was in addition to working a full-time job as a buyer and department manager for a busy retailer. Even when she came home from work, she busied herself with preparing home-cooked meals and cleaning the house. She also saw to it that we were in church every Sunday morning, Sunday night, and Wednesday night for services.

In her spare time, whatever there was of it, she and my dad took us to Gospel Quartet concerts in faraway cities and somehow managed to find time for trips to Disneyland and Knotts Berry Farm several times a year.

But none of that gave me one-on-one time with her. And I so desperately wanted it.

After my father passed away, I realized how unpredictable life can be. You never know how much time a loved one has left, and I didn't want my mother to leave this earth before I could make more memories with her. But simply longing for more one-on-one time with my mother wasn't getting me anywhere. Somehow, in some way, I had to make them happen while I still could. So, I made a plan. I knew my mother had always wanted to see Washington, DC, and now I was determined to take her. I discussed it with my husband, and he agreed to watch our sons while she and I went away for a few days to our nation's capital. Just the two of us, seeing all the legendary sights, shopping, eating out, and laughing together. That was one thing about my mother — she was fun. The only snag in my plan was her job. In the past, whenever I'd bring up the idea of taking a trip somewhere, she always said she couldn't take that much time off from work and all her other responsibilities.

But this time was different. I was on a mission.

I secretly called her boss at work and told him that I wanted to surprise my mother with a trip to Washington, DC. He was thrilled to be part of the surprise and said he'd schedule her the time off.

Next, I booked the place where we would stay, which was a former home of Robert Todd Lincoln in Georgetown. I even booked a limousine to pick us up at the airport once we landed. Everything was falling into place, down to the smallest detail. Now, I just had to get her to the airport for our pre-dawn flight.

On the morning of our departure, my husband and I drove over to her house and woke her up from a sound sleep. "What's going on?" she asked with half-open eyes.

"You need to pack because our plane to Washington, DC, leaves soon, and we need to be on it." When she realized the figure in her room wasn't going away, she stumbled out of bed and started to pack, all the while protesting how she couldn't possibly do whatever it was we were doing. I then explained I had already gotten everything cleared with her boss and the trip wasn't costing her anything. All she had to do was pack some clothes and get into the car. I also told her the plane tickets were non-refundable.

That's when she really started moving. My mother hated to see anyone lose money. She had watched her parents go through the depression, and she and my father had worked hard their whole lives to make ends meet. So, she wasn't about to let the perfectly good tickets go to waste. In fact, she was even starting to get excited.

Once we landed in Washington, DC, we made our way to baggage claim, where I knew the limousine driver would be waiting for us. She didn't know anything about that, though, so as we came down the escalator, she couldn't help but see the man in a dark suit standing at the bottom, holding a sign with my name on it and grinning a big, toothless smile.

Her first thought was I had lined her up with a blind date and she was having none of it. Once I explained who he was, she loved it.

The Robert Todd Lincoln home was wonderful. It was the headquarters of an organization I belonged to, and we had the house all to ourselves at night. But there was no elevator in the twenty-room mansion, and we had to walk up and down three flights of stairs every time we went anywhere. We ended up only staying the first night there, and then went to a hotel closer to the tourist attractions.

And we saw them all: the Washington Memorial, the Lincoln Memorial, Congress, the Smithsonian, Arlington cemetery, and more. My mother was having the time of her life, and I could barely keep up with her. The best part of the whole trip, though, was our conversations. I was loving every minute of them. My mom even picked up a couple of my books and started reading them out loud. And laughing! It felt good to be validated by someone whose sense of humor and work ethic I admired.

She asked questions about my work, and to my delight, she was getting to know the different, deeper, adult me, the *writer* me. Not that she hadn't supported me before. She had attended most of my plays, had all of my books, and laughed at my jokes. But this was different, deeper, and so fulfilling. I couldn't have been happier.

The surprise trip (almost a kidnapping) had been an overwhelming success. I made the memories I had been hoping for, and she got the trip she had dreamed about all her life. The memory-making didn't end there, though. That DC trip began a series of fun getaways for the two of us. They weren't long trips, just several days here and there to different places she wanted to see. They were fun, and they evolved into something even deeper than I had hoped. Instead of my mother getting to know me, I was getting to know her. And what a truly remarkable person she was. But I was right about life being unpredictable because only a couple of years later, my indefatigable mother was diagnosed with cancer and took her final journey, this time without me, to Heaven.

Today, whenever I recall that Washington, DC, trip or come across the dozens of photographs I took of us together there or on our other trips, I'm so glad I didn't just settle for wishing for the memories I wanted. Instead, I took the initiative and made the memories I'd always wanted. Memories I'll hold dear until Mom and I meet once more in that place where there'll be no more goodbyes.

Honor your father and mother—which is the first commandment with a promise— so that it may go well with you and that you may enjoy long life on the earth.

Ephesians 6:2-4 (NIV)

A Beauty-Licious Day

It's a beauty-licious day outside.
Miss Meadowlark told me so.
"A fine bodacious time to play,"
I heard her tell Old Crow.

Just scrump-dillyicious, thru-and-thru.
I'd get outside quick if I were you.
It's a dandy-delightful time to *be!*
To laugh and dance and grow.

It's an awesome majestic ride through life:
A matinee picture-show.
A charmingly-wonderful dash in time,
A breathtaking *tally-ho!*

Fun-dazzingly good just to be alive,
To hit a fly-ball! Or catch a line-drive!
A gorgeous-fantastic day has dawned,
So live it *grandissimo!*

Take My Breath Away

Rugged sculptured peaks ascending to the highest heavens,
Chiseled silhouettes against a vast ocean of sky,
And in the foothills, buried in an avalanche of sorrow,
One stone amidst the rubble lies concealed and asking, "Why?"
And I look up in awe to wonder how you even see me,
The grimiest of pebbles hidden from the light of day.
For I can't comprehend a grace so awesome in its favor,
A holy-righteous mountain, Lord, you take my breath away.

Magnificent Creator of the earth and sea and mountains,
Still sifting through the rock-pile and looking just for me,
You place me in your palm to gently blow away the chaffing,
Then set me in your Son to sparkle there for all to see.
Still I look up in awe and wonder how you ever saw me,
The tiniest of pebbles yet you knew just where I lay.
Yet I can't understand a God as close as my next whisper,
My Holy-Righteous Mountain, you still take my breath away.

Daddy Daughter Dance

"Dancing with the feet is one thing, but dancing with the heart is another."
Unknown

The hallmark of any truly great "watch-again" movie, in my opinion, is its ability to evoke laughter *and* tears. A case in point would be Steve Martin's *Father of the Bride.* Anyone who can watch this belly-buster romantic comedy without reaching for a Kleenex probably doesn't want to sit next to me, especially during the missed Daddy-Daughter Dance scene.

When my father was still alive, in a rare moment of intimacy while sitting beside him at my niece's wedding reception, he shared with me that his biggest regret in life was not being able to walk his three girls down the aisle on their wedding day. The crushing confusion, heartache, and "what ifs" of that longed for Daddy-Daughter Dance on my wedding day can still summon wistful whimsies of liquid love.

I didn't think much of the omission when my husband and I tied the knot in December 1970. There had been so much pain in my house growing up: yelling, hitting, cursing, baiting, drinking . . . and then, the hardship of no child support after the divorce and my mother trying to raise four kids on a dime.

In post WWII America, divorce was considered taboo. Shameful and degrading, especially in Roman Catholic circles. So when I overheard my little friend's grandma tell her she couldn't play with me because my family was trash, I shamefaced away and spent years trying to overcome that despicable declaration over me and my family.

When planning my wedding — actually, my youngest sister, Debbie, did most of the legwork because I was teaching in the opposite corner of the state — as always, I was just trying to keep the peace in my family, a role I often played throughout the years. I couldn't stand to see my mother in tears, a response that my dad's presence was quick to evoke in her.

Loud, boisterous, and obnoxious, Dad was a Navy Veteran of WWII, the repercussions on the human psyche of which I didn't even begin to grasp at the time. As a result, I cringed in fear and dread, even as a child, when he'd burst through the back kitchen door, home from work.

Later, as a young teen, when it was my delegated duty to beg for two quarters so my sister Suzie and I could go roller-skating on a Sunday afternoon, I'd get sick to my stomach at the thought of approaching him. I remember standing off to his side as he "read the newspaper," ignoring me, knowing full well I was there. He also knew what I wanted but pretended ignorance, intent on making this weekly ordeal as miserable as possible.

Suzie jabbed at me from behind. "Go on!"

Shuffling my feet, head down, I corner-eyed him. *Come on, Donna, you can do this. You've done it dozens of times.* Still, my heart thumping against my chest felt like a mallet beating a bass drum. I sucked in a breath and cleared my throat. "Dad?"

No answer.

I tried again, this time with more *oomph*. "Dad?"

Finally, tossing the paper aside, he'd acknowledge my presence. "Yeah? What do you want now?" I knew he *knew* my intent, and although he usually relented after giving me the third degree, this ritual and similar encounters left a crippling scar on our ability to communicate in later years.

You didn't *talk* to my dad.

You listened.

Even years later, on a long-distance telephone call with him, I'd catch myself wearing a stupid jack-o-lantern grin, still trying to please him even though he couldn't see me.

So, in the whirlwind of planning my wedding ceremony and reception, when it came to the finer points of decision making, I readily understood why my mother didn't want him there. I didn't want any trouble either.

Consequently, the traditional walk down the aisle and Daddy-Daughter Dance went to my new stepfather, a man barely older than myself. A "daddy replacement" who I would later learn wasn't just making inappropriate nuances toward me when I was home from college breaks but was provoking my two younger sisters into misery as well.

Only in more recent years, after viewing the new 2001 movie *Pearl Harbor* and similar war films, did I begin to get a glimpse of the hell Dad and thousands of other young men had endured. I began to understand the scars of the horrific war. Mental wounds, as well as physical scars like the jagged place in his left calf riddled with shrapnel from a crazed Kamikaze pilot diving into the bridge of his ship.

Marriage to a wonderful guy helped heal some of my own mental scars. My opinion of myself radically changed when I gave my heart to Jesus in the fall of 1973 and realized I was a Child of the King. After that, I tried to approach Dad many times about seeking a personal relationship with the Lover of His Soul, but he always cut me off before I could get the words out of my mouth. "Oh yeah," he'd say, *talking* with his hands flailing, as was his habit. "I took care of that stuff a long time ago."

"What 'stuff,' Dad?"

He hesitated only slightly. "Hell, just cuz I can't go to mass," — the Roman Catholic Church excommunicated divorcees back then — "I still say my altar-boy prayers in Latin and watch Mass on TV."

Then, like a racehorse, he'd be off again, babbling meaningless gibberish. Anything to keep the conversation in his control—until one fateful day, thirty-three years after our missed Daddy-Daughter Dance.

My breath caught in my throat at the heartbreaking sight playing out before my eyes like an old 1940s newsreel. The crackling flames and homey heat radiating from Cracker Barrel's oversized fireplace that day did little to warm the cold dread gripping my heart as I watched my brother help my father navigate the maze of tables to our reserved spot. Even aided by the three-pronged cane he was using, Dad could barely walk.

Hugs and welcoming words aside, my family all settled down for an almost home-cooked meal. While we tried to visit with each other, as always, Dad seemed to suck the air from the room with his nonstop brassy banter:

Flirting with our young waitress, "You're good lookin' Chickee! Watcha got cookin'?"

Griping his displeasure with the Chicago Cubs: "*Ahhh*, they're blankety-blank useless! So-and-so couldn't hit a blankety-blank ball spoon-fed to him by his own mother."

Sharing his sinus problems with anyone who would care to hear . . . or not: "This blankety-blank snot I'm constantly getting out my sinuses is blankety-blank-blank!" He paused to blow his nose, the sound resembling a bawling elephant. "I don't know where this blankety-blank stuff comes from anyway!"

Finally . . . it was time to leave. My brother Donnie helped him with his heavy winter jacket, handed him his walking cane, and, with a great show of effort, huddled Dad outdoors to bundle him into the waiting car.

But, as Dad and I embraced each other in a farewell hug, to my surprise, he held on tight. "Please pray for me, Honey," he whispered in a cracked voice. "I never thought I'd get to this."

I cried all the way home.

One month later, I got a phone call saying he was at Death's Door. Speeding all 120 miles, I prayed fervently: "Please, God, don't let him die before I get there."

The Lord answered my prayer. Not only that, but He made sure Dad was the only one in the room when I arrived. And so, in the solitude of a sterile, lonely place — with machines bleeping, whooshing, and clicking — lacking only my bridal gown and a dance band, Dad and I finally "danced" the waltz we'd missed on my wedding day.

Sitting on the edge of his bed, as I held his once strong hand against my wet cheek, we swayed together while I sang familiar 1950s love songs. Then, finally, whispering my forgiveness and love into his ear, I took the chance I'd been hoping for all my adult life. "Daddy, I want to be with you again in Heaven. Forever. Would you like to ask Jesus into your heart?"

Unable to talk, his eyes intently held mine for a long moment. Then . . . he nodded. And right then and there, Heaven's angels had a party as my father finally accepted the invitation to dance forever with his Savior.

As we ended our prayer that day, Dad squeezed my hand and closed his eyes. I sang one final song:

Anchors Aweigh, my boy,
Anchors Aweigh.
Farewell to foreign shores,
you sail at break of day . . .
Though your last night ashore,
where 'er you roam,
Until we meet once more,
here's wishing you a happy voyage home.

Even in laughter the heart may be in pain, and the end of joy may be grief.

Proverbs 14:13 (NAS)

I fled Him down the nights and down the days.

I fled Him, down the arches of the years.

I fled Him, down the labyrinthine ways

Of my own mind; and in the midst of tears.

—"The Hound of Heaven" —
(Francis Thompson, 1859-1907)

Permanent Houseguest

Hound of Heaven, pursue my friend; sandpaper-kiss her face
To coax her giggle, restore her soul, to slather her with grace
That tempts her heart with squirming, wiggly-waggly puppy whines
As balm to heal the wounds and hurts provoked by Hell's designs

To cripple and ensnare her in deceptions of the past,
The lies of devils meant to keep her prisoner and outcast,
When all she yearns for is to feel the warmth of your sweet breath.
Track down my friend, with panting thirst, who's hitchhiking with death.

Keep scampering, yelping, yipping and nip-nipping at her heels
To trip her up and knock her down until she finally kneels,
Reminding her she's royalty, this princess in disguise,
Who wrestles with the Hound-of-Love through tears of blinded eyes.

Entice her, please, to hug you close, embrace your racing heart,
Forgetting and forgiving all that's tearing her apart,
Adoring as a newborn babe to nestle in your rest,
To snuggle, and invite you stay as permanent houseguest.

Thanks for the Memories

by Martha Bolton

"I grew up with six brothers.
That's how I learned to dance — waiting for the bathroom."
Bob Hope

It was the event Hollywood had been waiting for—Bob Hope's 90th birthday—and family, friends, and fans were excited to celebrate it in a big way. NBC was pulling out all the stops. They would air a three-hour primetime television special boasting a roster of A-list guest stars. Some of the celebrities featured on the show were Carol Burnett, George Burns, Garth Brooks, Jimmy Stewart, Johnny Carson, Rosemary Clooney, Phyllis Diller, Ginger Rogers, Raquel Welch, and Presidents Nixon, Carter, Bush, Ford, and Clinton . . . And the list went on.

There was even a pre-show, taped on a different date, in front of NBC studios and hosted by Jay Leno. I brought along my pastor and our youth group to be in the audience for that taping, which also featured a military flyover.

In addition, for a television special appropriately titled *Bob Hope—the First 90 Years*, Bob's wife Dolores threw a private 90th birthday party in their backyard. It was at that party that I had my One Chance . . . One Dance moment. When I saw that Ronald Reagan was in attendance, I decided I would do whatever I could to meet him. He had been a guest on some of the specials I had written for, and fellow Bob Hope writer Doug Gamble was on Reagan's speechwriting team. Besides all that, he was a former and beloved president. Who wouldn't want to meet him?

Unfortunately, every time I tried to get close to him, other fans or the Secret Service moved in around him, and my plans were thwarted. Finally, I told my husband to take a photo if I ever got close enough that it even appeared like we were talking. But then, that plan didn't work either.

When they gave the call for dinner, and we all began to make our way to the giant white tent that had been set up, I found myself on the walkway, walking directly behind Ronald Reagan. I picked up my pace and caught up to him. "Mr. President," I said. "Would you mind taking your picture with me?" To my amazement, he agreed to do it! It was early evening, rather dark, but our camera had a flash, so I was certainly happy about that. The president and I struck a pose, then smiled at the camera that my husband was nervously holding. But the flash did not go off! I was so disappointed. But then, President Reagan turned to me and asked if I'd like to try it again. I couldn't believe it! The president was giving my discount camera a reprieve. We struck another pose, smiled again, and once again *the flash did not go off.*

Embarrassed, I genuinely thanked him, and let him move along toward the seating area. The next morning, hoping against hope that something had registered on the film, I took the roll to be developed. To my disappointment, nothing showed up. It was just a black negative. But I went ahead and had an enlargement made of it, framed it, and hung it on my wall.

Why, you may ask? Simple. *Because I knew* it was me and Ronald Reagan, and even the blank picture seemed to help take the pain out of my lost "One Chance . . . One Dance" moment.

But then . . . one night I was giving a speech and recounting this story for the audience. It was one of my favorite stories and always gets a good laugh.

But after the event a man approached me and asked, "So did you ever get that picture?"

"No," I said. "I had my two chances, and I blew it." Then, the man reached into his pocket and pulled out a business card, saying, "Well, maybe I can help." He handed me the card, and I quickly read it. It said, "Michael Reagan." It was President Reagan's son!

The following week, I received a call from Ronald Reagan's office, inviting me and my entire family to meet him and have our photographs taken. After passing through layer after layer of security, we were finally escorted into his office. We talked briefly. Then his photographer took a picture of me with him, my husband with him, and each of my sons with him, and then all of us together.

President Reagan even shared his own sense of humor when he showed us a souvenir he had on his desk. "It's a tool for dealing with Congress," he said. Then, he humorously demonstrated the wooden block. "See here? You can turn it at different angles to reveal the words, *Yes*, *No*, and *Scram*." We all shared a good laugh, and it was a wonderful memory for my family.

The presidential visit had turned out a lot better than I could have ever hoped, all because I'd decided to laugh at my "missed chance" and then shared that misadventure with an audience one serendipitous evening. In turn—at least one man among them—reciprocated by giving me my one opportunity to change that disappointing photo-op.

For sometimes, that one missed chance does find its way back to hug your heart in a brand-new happy dance. "Thank you, Lord! And thank you, Bob Hope. Thanks for the memories."

You did it: you changed wild lament into whirling dance; You ripped off my
black mourning band and decked me with wildflowers. I'm about to burst
with song; I can't keep quiet about you.
God, my God, I can't thank you enough.

Psalms 30:11-12 (TM)

photo courtesy of Martha Bolton

Make You Famous

I want to make you famous, Lord, in everything I do:
To take the limelight off myself and shine it unto you,
To live you loud, and sing your song, and dance your grand ballet;
To empty me, and let you fill this fragile jar of clay.

I want to make you famous, Lord, in everything I say:
To speak your heart, anoint my lips, to offer life today,
To whisper hope and shout your truth with kindness as my guide;
To lay me down upon the cross to crucify my pride.

I want to make you famous, Lord, in everything I think:
To pour a cup of mercy, offering living water's drink;
To cast aside the hurts I feel, while choosing to forgive,
To cleanse me from the inside out to worship and to live.

I want to make you famous, Lord, in every step I take:
To follow paths, you chart before me, for your own Name's sake.
To live with purpose, strength, and power that others will embrace;
To script a sermon with my life of your amazing grace.

I want to make you famous, Lord, in everything I pray:
To offer up my sacrifice, a sweet, perfumed bouquet;
To enter thru the Gates of Praise, beyond this broken mirror,
To see reflections of the day you'll wipe away each tear.

I Want To Hold Your Hand

"Hand in hand, we dance through life, embracing the rhythm of our hearts."
Uknown

My stepdad was just beginning to come out of the anesthetic after a major heart surgery. As I watched Don slowly regain consciousness, before he even opened his eyes, I was touched when the first thing he did was to reach for my mother's hand, who was waiting, standing beside his post-operative bed. It was a simple act, yet so profound — this straightforward, spontaneous reflex. It seemed to say, "I need you; I love you; I'm so glad you're here for me."

Intimacy. For many in our 21st. Century hurry-up, immediate gratification microwave society, this word conjures up nothing but the out-of-touch with reality, hurried bedroom scene with someone you may or may not really know: Jack meets Jane. Jane likes Jack. Jane goes to bed with Jack. Jack leaves Jane. Goes looking for a new Jane while Jane goes looking for a new Jack.

Unfortunately, many of today's young people have little concept of "romance." How could they when every movie they watch, song they listen to, and even TV commercials, intentionally placed between sitcoms and weekend sporting events, drums Satan's all-prevailing lie into their psyches that "Love" is somehow synonymous with "Sex." I contend that while making love is the God-given, ultimate intimate act between a man and a woman, the art of simple old-fashioned handholding is far more endearing and meaningful in the long run.

I remember the first time my husband reached for my hand. It was our maiden voyage: the first dress-up, go-out-to-eat, and catch-a-movie date night, when we set sail for the Circle Theatre in downtown Indianapolis, IN, to see *The Sound Of Music*.

Somewhere between "Climb Every Mountain" and "I Must Have Done Something Good," I felt Barry not-so-nonchalantly span the short distance between our two galleys to tentatively grasp my hand and then hold on for dear life.

I didn't breathe for a few seconds as I kept my eyes focused on Julie Andrews up on the big screen, happily singing with the Von Trapp children: "Do, a deer, a female deer. Re, a drop of golden sun. Mi, a name I call myself . . ."

Slowly, I relaxed and let my cold wooden fingers curl into his warm, welcoming hand. We fit together perfectly, and we've never let go. Holding hands is still how we go to sleep every night. I don't remember exactly when we started this ritual, but I cherish it. One I miss on the rare occasions when life has called one or the other of us away from home for the evening.

I was an awkward, keep-your-eyes-down, don't-talk-to-me freshman in high school when The Beatles' hit single "I Want To Hold Your Hand" first hit the pop charts. Back then, it seemed that the whole school would gather daily in the high school lobby after lunch, where the girls would dance with each other while the boys watched.

To a starry-eyed teeny-bopper, Paul McCartney's and John Lennon's winsome lyrics conjured up daydreams of romance as they sang, "Oh, I'll tell you something I think you'll understand. When I say that something, I want to hold your hand . . ." Of course, we girls instinctively understood what that "something" was and dreamed of the day when one special boy would say, "I love you," to us.

In a 2008 study of how human touch affects neural stress release, Jim Coan, an assistant professor in the University of Virginia's psychology department, conducted extensive research on the brain and found that when couples held hands, the wife experienced less pain during an electric shock if they had their husband's hand intertwined with theirs, rather than that of a stranger. Or no hand at all.

"In a happy marriage," Coan said, "Women who hold their husbands' hands feel instant relief from stressful situations. We're calling them 'super couples' because they are so off the charts happy!"

Furthermore, Tom DeMaio, a clinical psychologist who counsels pairs in the Charlottesville area, even went so far as to say he often recommends to couples he's working with that they hold hands during a fight. "It keeps them connected when trying to work things out during tough times."

Speaking of connecting, nothing says loving better than holding each other's hands to pray together as husband and wife. I remember like it was yesterday when Barry and I first tried it. I felt embarrassed. No doubt, he did, too. But to this day, I still cherish that naked feeling of absolute vulnerability and transparency in opening my heart to the Creator of the Universe in front of my husband while holding his hand.

Earlier that Saturday afternoon, we'd both given our hearts to Jesus while participating in a "Lay Witness Mission," a ministry where ordinary people like you and me come into a community to share how Jesus Christ personally changed their lives to turn them upside-down and inside-out.

Originally, we'd been less than thrilled when we learned that Barry's mother, who was in charge of locating homes for the visitors to spend the weekend, had volunteered our house.

"What?" Barry groaned. "Mom, I don't want to spend the whole weekend in church!"

I wholeheartedly agreed with him. "You're kidding, right?"

After all, we had our own lives to live: going out with friends, hanging out on our couches in front of the TV, sleeping in Saturday mornings, and later walking uptown to our favorite coney dog restaurant . . .

Being schoolteachers at the time — me teaching fifth grade, and Barry, the high school band director — church attendance to us was merely the "right thing to do." As American as apple pie. Something we did to keep in good standing with the Man upstairs — if, indeed, there was a God. Going to church on Sundays afforded us a pleasant "religious experience," to say the least.

Now, holding hands as we knelt together at the feet of Jesus on our new 1970s moss-green shag carpeting, we swallowed our awkwardness and took a deep breath. Barry took my hand to begin: "Dear Lord, we come to you together as husband and wife to ask you to use us together to further your Kingdom of Love in whatever way you see fit . . ."

Those simple, tentative, yet sincere words pouring from his soul that day were so intense, raw, heartfelt, and engaging that I started crying. But as those tears freely flowed, bathed in the awe of this new experience, I never felt closer to my husband. A fact that still holds true to this day whenever we join hands to talk to God.

I'm convinced that only one difference separates successful, loving marriages from those that end in a shipwreck. One unrelenting pied-piper lures thousands of unsuspecting couples to the divorce courts while playing various renditions of the same song in different rhythms and keys, over and over again.

Pride.

Holding hands to pray together destroys this mangy monster quicker than anything I've ever experienced. Walls of un-forgiveness, anger, and self-centeredness all crumble as we enter the King of Kings' throne room, holding hands to say:

"I'm sorry."

"Will you forgive me?"

"I was wrong . . ."

Even if we're not feeling it, these humble words naturally flow from a thawing heart in the presence of the One who knows us better than we know ourselves to usher in healing, restoration, and forgiveness.

I remember trying to explain this principle to a group of teenage girls one day after a brutal dance team practice because they were all squabbling. Fiery mad at each other — snarling, bawling, and clawing at each other's feelings in the way only self-centered adolescent girls can.

"Look, just make yourself say you're sorry!" I'd suggested at the closing team meeting, "It doesn't matter what you're feeling. 'I'm sorry' will bring healing."

"So, you're saying we should lie, Mrs. Frisinger?" one of the underclassmen protested in outrage.

"No!" I rolled my eyes in frustration. These immature, "me-myself, and I," pony-tailed high-kickers weren't buying what I was laying down. "What I'm saying is, if you take that first step to say you're sorry, you'll find that it brings about reconciliation to throw a wet towel on both party's anger."

They looked at me like I'd just told them to remove their ears and screw them on backward.

Although their reaction that day wasn't what I'd hoped for, years later one of those girls approached me one day in the grocery store to thank me for suggesting the impossible to her then adolescent mind. "It really works, Mrs. Frisinger," she said, hugging me. "My husband and I have been married ten years and have always followed your advice."

In the end, it doesn't matter, does it? Who's right? Who's wrong? What matters is friendship. What matters is family. What matters is love.

In humbling ourselves to say, "I'm sorry," or "I'm sorry, too," — closed doors swing open wide to usher in healing, hugs, and humility to produce Love. A "staying love" that is real, not here today and gone tomorrow, but genuine love.

A scene from *The Velveteen Rabbit* by Margery Williams, is the magical conversation when the Skin Horse describes 'real love' to a newly arrived stuffed bunny:

The Skin Horse had lived longer in the nursery than any of the others. He was so old that his brown coat was bald in patches and showed the seams underneath, and most of the hairs in his tail had been pulled out to string bead necklaces.

He was wise, for he had seen a long succession of mechanical toys arrive to boast and swagger, and by-and-by break their mainsprings and pass away, and he knew they were only toys and would never turn into anything else . . .

". . . What is REAL?" asked the Velveteen Rabbit one day . . . Does it mean having things that buzz inside you and a stick-out handle?"

"REAL isn't how you are made," said the Skin Horse. "It's a thing that happens to you. When a child "really loves" you a long, long time, not just to play with, but really loves you, then you become REAL"

"Does it hurt?" asked the Rabbit.

"Sometimes," said the Skin Horse, for he was always truthful. "When you are REAL, you don't mind being hurt."

"Does it happen all at once, like being wound up," he asked, "or bit by bit."

"It doesn't happen all at once," said the Skin Horse. "You become. It takes a long time. That's why it doesn't often happen to people who break easily, or have sharp edges, or have to be carefully kept. Generally, by the time you are REAL, most of you hair has been loved off, and your eyes drop out and you get loose in the joints and very shabby. But these things don't matter at all, because once you are REAL you can't be ugly, except to people who don't understand."

REAL: that's how I feel when Barry and I hold hands. Sometimes, I can't even tell where his hand starts and mine begins. We are one, as God meant us to be: ". . . And when I touch you, I feel happy inside . . ."

For I, the Lord your God, hold your right hand; it is I who says to you,
"Fear not, I am the one who helps you."

Isaiah 41:13-14 (ESV)

I found him who my soul loves. Song of Solomon 3:4 (ESV)

Our Sandcastle

We started our sandcastle
In the springtime of our vows,
Just a bucketful of hope
Sifted from the Sea of Life,

Not a manual with instructions
Or a predetermined plan
With a blueprint for tomorrow
When I said I'd be your wife.

And we added to it daily:
Towers to see beyond today,
Framing walls that would secure
Our chosen ground.

Filling moats with tears we shed
In breathless laughter and raw pain,
Building bridges
For securing what we found.

Knowing one day our castle
Would vanish with the wind,
To be washed away
In frothy, crashing foam.
And no one would recall
The dreams we built upon this shore
on that day
When you and I will be called home.

So, we built to leave a legacy,
To live in such a way,
That the world may want to borrow
What we found:
Far more real than gold or silver
Or the plans that mortals make,
Storing treasures in the coves
Of Love's Playground.

To find strength to face tomorrow
As we sought the face of God,
Felt such tenderness
It seemed our hearts would break.
Sang and danced upon our seashore
Self-assured in what we found:
Treasured friendship, solemn trust
Through give-and-take.

We found feathers left by seagulls
And they gave us wings to fly,
Felt the sun
While strolling barefoot on the beach.
Chased the waves from rolling tides
In lovers' never-ending songs,
Stretched for sand dollars and shells
Beyond our reach.

And it was grand,
Building, hand-in-hand,
A woman and her man.

Twinkle Toes: Matty's Twirly-Whirly

"Twinkle Toes:" That's what we nicknamed him. A twirly-whirly bundle of joy. And holy cannoli, this kid loved to dance.

Do you believe in love at first sight? Your answer may depend on what that first sight is focused on. Or better yet, who it's focused on? For my husband Barry, the surprising object of a new affection was a bouncing baby boy named Matty.

Matty and Mommy, my nineteen-year-old niece, had come to live with us shortly after he was born. By the time Matty was old enough to push himself up to a standing position to gurgle, "Up!" the deal had been sealed — a God-ordained love affair began. A bond so deep that the connection between the two of them can still take Barry's breath away at times. A feeling so profound that it physically hurts when he has to say "Goodbye" to this little boy on days he comes to visit.

Only God knows exactly when this softhearted love affair of the soul began. Maybe it was the first time Barry held the sweet-smelling baby boy in his arms to feed him his bottle. Or perhaps when he cradled that infant, singing silly ditties, when Matty fussed, sick with fever. Or when Mommy needed a break from the constant needs of a newborn to take a much-desired shower.

If you ask my husband, however, he'll probably say it was the first time he'd abandoned his usual "must-have," first-cup-of-coffee morning ritual to glance down our kitchen steps to see Matty wobbly-bobbling at the gate we'd erected across the bottom step of our basement so he couldn't climb up and take a tumble.

Matty and Mommy lived downstairs back then, where we'd removed the door at the top of the stairwell to make it seem more open. Upon seeing Barry, framed in his big blue-eyed expectant vision, peering down at him from the top of the stairs like a new golden retriever puppy craving the touch of his owner's affection, Matty would lift his chubby cherub arms in an eye-sparkling gurgling plea that seemed to say, "Come get me, 'Bawwy.' ("R's" are hard to pronounce for little ones.) "Rescue me from this baffling, barred prison!"

And the man was hooked.

"Can I come get Matty and bring him upstairs?" he'd call down the steps.

"Sure," a groggy but willing voice would answer, as any totally exhausted new mother would.

Kazaam! From that point on, man and baby were inseparable. Where Barry went, Matty followed. Where Matty explored, Barry explored. What Matty watched on TV, Barry watched: "Blue's Clues," "Thomas the Train," "Paw Patrol . . . "

Then came the delightful day when Barry flipped on our stereo to play Mannheim Steamrollers' synthesized version of Handel's "Halleluiah Chorus." A piece of music so anointed when Handel was composing his 13th. Century "Messiah" masterpiece, friends found him weeping, closed up in his room, and refusing to come out until the work was done. It seems the 64-year-old Handel was so overcome with the awesome majesty of his new work he later said, "I did think I saw all Heaven before me and the great God himself."

The first time Matty heard Handel's masterpiece, Magic flooded our living room carpet. He stood stock still for a moment, mesmerized by what he was hearing. Then he squealed, gurgling gleefully, and for the first time began strutting what we later called his "twinkle-toes" promenade. A light-footed, baby boogie-woogie.

First, he bounced up and down in time to the driving beat of the music. Then, much to our delight, he clapped along with us as we encouraged him to explore his newfound feelings. Finally, Matty gleefully stomped in a wonky-wobbly circle and, in our eyes, at least, a young Fred Astaire was born.

From that first dance until Matty and Mommy moved out, all four of us would routinely march, twirl, laugh, and boogie-down to Handel's old-but-new 17th-century masterpiece. Hoofing it up like crazy people, we'd encourage him in his twirls, stomps, and seemingly perfect pauses until today, Matty's dancing has morphed into his own unique break-dance-styled hoedown.

As someone who has been immersed in music since childhood, I've always been amazed at how Matty can "read" and interpret the dance hidden inside a piece of music, even to the point of "freezing" in places when the song calls for it. Today, now joined by two younger brothers, Sammy and Wiley, he still clamors to show off his latest move when he comes to visit.

"Hey Barry," he might say today, popping through the front door along with his siblings, "I've got some new moves to show you." At which point, we all gather around to be suitably astonished by his newest concoction of dance steps. One of the last times he visited, Matty astounded us when he bowed his head to run faster, faster, faster . . . in a continuous, spot-on tight circle to then freeze his body abruptly into a karate-chop statue.

Then, Sammy and Wiley begin their clamor for equal attention. "Now, watch ours!" And so it begins: the dual to outdo each other.

Sadly, today, Matty and his brothers are going through more heartache than any little boy should have to endure. Following the heartache of Divorce, Matty's daddy has died; he's lived in multiple houses, been embroiled in classroom troubles, is now changing schools, and dealing with contrary emotions he has no idea how to deal with. Rules that don't seem fair, and seemingly no steady foundation to anchor his anger.

But . . . there *is* Prayer.

Every day, sometimes in the middle of the night from tear-stained pillows, our constant plea is that Matty will continue to boogie-down, holding hands with "The Lord of the Dance," all his lifelong days. And we pray that the dance of his childhood never stops but whirls on and on throughout his life until Kingdom-Come, when we'll all be dancing in a circle of merriment together around the Throne Room of our God, where all toes will twinkle.

Jesus said, "Let the little children come to me, and do not hinder them, for the kingdom of heaven belongs to such as these."

Matthew 19:14 (NIV)

For everything there is a season, and a time for every matter under heaven: a time to be born, and a time to die; . . . a time to weep, and a time to laugh; . . . a time to mourn, and a time to dance; Ecclesiastes 3:1-4 (ESV)

Perfectly Precious You

Are you perfect, Cheeky-Child?
Fiercely free and wonder-wild.
Heaven clapped the day you smiled . . .
You're my precious cheeky child.

Are you perfect, Twinkle-Toes?
Tapping, twirling dancing shows,
Even when the music slows . . .
You're my precious twinkle toes.

Are you perfect, Funny-Face?
Chugga-chugga choo-choo chase,
Race into your secret place.
You're my precious funny face.

Are you perfect, Clapping-Clown?
Stack a tower — knock it down.
"Pick your toys up!" Big! Fat! Frown!
You're my precious clapping clown.

Are you perfect, Boo-Hoo-Bear?
Snuffling in your time-out chair,
You're not going *anywhere* . . .
You're my precious boo-hoo bear.

Are you perfect, Buckaroo?
"Ride'em, Cowboy!" Me and you
Round up critters from the zoo.
You're my precious buckaroo.

Are you perfect, Silly-Pickle?
Bellybutton — tummy tickle.
Giggle, wiggle, fussy, fickle,
You're my precious silly pickle.

Are you perfect, Jelly-Fish?
Ships-ahoy, Mate. Swirly-swish.
Snorkeling! Bubbling! Squiggly-*squishhh!*
You're my precious jelly fish.

Are you perfect, Cuddle-Bug?
Read our books, then squeezy-hug.
Giggle, wiggle, tickle, tug.
You're my precious cuddle-bug.

Are you perfect, Peek-a-Boo?
You're God's gift and I love you.
Every day we start brand new.
You're my precious peek-a-boo.

Are you perfect, Sleepyhead?
"Nighty-night," tucked tight in bed.
Moonlight whispers overhead,
"You're my precious sleepyhead."

Caboose Crossroads

by Martha Bolton

"The moment is everything. Don't think about tomorrow; don't think about yesterday: think about exactly what you're doing right now and live it, dance it, breathe it, and be it."
Martha Graham

My hands trembled with both excitement and trepidation as I turned to Page 2 of my hometown newspaper. Sure enough, it was there. Only it wasn't in the Letters to the Editor Section, as I had expected. It was listed under the heading of Guest Columnist.

When You're Done in By a Caboose was the title of a satirical piece I had written about how trains would often cut our community in half by parking on the tracks and blocking traffic.

My "guest column" focused on this one particular day when, after what seemed like an eternity, I turned around and tried a different street, only to have the train take off and beat me there. And then, it parked.

When I tried to go back to the street it had just vacated, it backed up and beat me to that street, too. And parked yet again.

It became one of those situations in life that was so frustrating that it actually turned comical. I decided to put my angst to good use and write about it.

Ever since I was a young girl, I have loved to write. I wrote poems that I taped to the wall next to my bed, and entered a gag-writing contest when I was fourteen years old.

Throughout my teens I wrote essays and short stories, and an article here and there, but seeing my name in a "Guest Column" in the town newspaper felt like I had reached a new level.

For the next few days, I watched the paper to see if there would be any comments in the *Letters to the Editor* section. There were a few, which made me feel good to know that people had enjoyed my writing.

Until. . . the afternoon when I picked up the paper from the shrubbery where the paperboy had thrown it and I opened to page 2 and saw a comment that made my heart sink.

Printed there for the whole town to see was a scathing retort to my Guest Column. Missing all sense of satire, the letter writer scolded me for writing about the trains. Didn't I realize how much trains have done for our country? And on and on it went. It ended with: "Martha Bolton, I hope you never write again!"

I was crushed, discouraged, and confused. Putting my writing out there had been a huge mistake. What was I thinking anyway? My words were safer taped to the wall by my bed than appearing anywhere in public.

I wiped my tears and packed away my typewriter, telling myself I was better off never trying *that* again.

And yet, something inside wouldn't let me deny my love of writing. I wouldn't be me if I didn't have a pen in my hand. Why was I letting one mean-spirited critic, who'd probably had their own bad day, take that away from me?

I came up with a plan. I'd use a pen name—M. Boulton. Not a big disguise, but enough to give me some protection. I then called the editor and asked if I could submit another piece for the paper. He was very open to the idea, and we even discussed a regular column.

But after a few months of writing as M. Boulton, and becoming more comfortable with the process, I told the editor I'd prefer to use my real name again. He was happy to make the change but asked why I had wanted to use a pen name in the first place.

I reminded him about that one letter to the editor, and he just laughed, "Oh, that? That was just a twelve-year-old boy."

I couldn't believe how close I came to giving up on any kind of a writing career simply because of the hurtful words of a kid who didn't even know me, and had probably never even given another thought to me or that article again.

My fears could have easily made that my last dance. But my passion for writing would not let go of me. With my real name back in place and a lot less timidity, I decided to go for it. I set writing goals and made sure I met them. I took writing classes and entered contests. I tried my hand at all different writing genres, from articles to playwriting, speechwriting, books, and greeting cards.

Since comedy was my forte, I began writing for different comedians, including legendary comedy legends Phyllis Diller and Joan Rivers. From there I was recommended to Bob Hope, and became his first woman staff writer, writing for his primetime television specials, military shows, and personal appearances for approximately fifteen years.

Has it all been easy? Not at all. It's been a lot of work. And I still get occasional disappointments and discouraging comments. But I've received far more positive reinforcement.

I've been blessed to have been nominated for an Emmy, a Dove Award, and a Writers Guild Award, and am the playwright for "Blue Gate Musicals LLC," with over a dozen musicals in our repertory, including two based on novels I have written. My eighty-ninth book, which was released in 2021, was *Dear Bob . . . Bob Hope's Wartime Correspondence with the GIs of WWII.* My writing has taken me into the company of Hollywood celebrities, sports legends, and political figures, including several presidents. But I would have missed it all had I listened to my fears and not taken another chance at a writing career. I took that chance, and there's been no looking back.

Jesus said to him, "No one who puts his hand to the plow and looks back is fit for the kingdom of God."

Luke 9:62 (ESV)

Magic Waiting Room

There is a land above the trees
Where alpine tundra grow,
A place where God still walks the earth
To view Creation's show,

While turning His kaleidoscope
Of ever-present change,
In panoramic theaters
Of endless mountain range.

It's here I find balm for my soul,
Refreshment, peace and pardon,
While drinking in the wonder of
His Majesty's rock garden

From ancient stepping-stones that lie
Upon this hallowed peak,
Where pollinating, buzzing bees
Are playing hide-and-seek

With nectars pooled in potpourris
Of petals in full-bloom,
Just one step down from Heaven
In this "Magic Waiting Room."

Masterpiece

"To dance, put your hand on your heart and listen to the sound of your soul."
Eugene Louis Faccuito

The black silhouette is perfectly cast against the early-morning sunrise. Two fishermen, captured in the framed camera lens of my eye, are sitting perfectly still in their small boat, their fishing lines taunt as the converging blues and purples of the past evening overlap the bright oranges and yellows of the emerging sunrise from the water's rim. And I remember the first time I was introduced to pastel chalk.

I was in the eighth grade at St. Joseph's parochial school in Dyer, IN, when Sister Claire Marie, our daunting, demanding teacher, passed out a plain white sheet of 12x18 construction paper to each of her forty-six students. While there were no class-size limits in those days, Sister had no trouble maintaining discipline. When she went into one of her tirades, everyone quaked in dread, at least in their imagination, while holding on to their ears.

You see, Sister had the dreadful habit of pulling a mischievous student out of their seat by the ear, grimacing and clenching her teeth to croak her guttural rage: "I told you not to . . ." the sentence to be completed with whatever dire behavior had prompted her outburst.

Classmate Bobby Reese could imitate her perfectly, which he often did whenever she'd leave the room, drawing gales of giggles from the rest of us.

Now Sister proceeded to open a large mysterious tin box taken from the bottom drawer of her desk. "For our Art Lesson today, we'll learn how to use pastel chalk." She had my full attention as she explained the technique for using this new coloring medium. Friday's Art Class was my very favorite part of the school week, and this was something brand new I'd never tried before.

"You hold the chalk piece on its side," she continued. "Unlike crayons, the beauty of working with chalk comes from blending the various colors together, using your fingertips." She demonstrated, then explained the second phase of our project that day: to draw and then cut a silhouette of any object we desired from the black construction paper she would provide to glue it onto our completed chalk background.

I immediately knew what I wanted to do as I covered my entire paper in dark blues and purples. I then overlapped this rather dark, drab background to work in oranges, reds, and yellows to form an arch of piercing rays that extended out to the paper's edges from the center as I deftly worked the colors together with my fingertips before adding black, gray and brown shades to form a rocky hill in the lower foreground.

Now, I was ready for the silhouette I had in mind. Cutting out three black construction paper crosses, one larger than the other two, I carefully glued them onto the chalk background atop my foreboding hill. Mission accomplished. In my mind it was a chalk rendition of the darkness and light which is Calvary's paradox.

But even recalling that long-ago art project, I am drawn to yet another chalk memory. This time, I was a junior in high school and had been asked to draw the murals for our Junior-Senior Prom, "Southern Enchantment."

Remembering my previous infatuation with the pastels, I decided to color these huge background drawings with chalk. Only I would use oil chalk this time to give the murals the illusion of massive oil paintings.

Brilliant! What I didn't consider, however, was the necessity of blending the oil chalk into the large frescos with bare fingers, which my fellow classmates and I did nightly in the confines of my basement. We even skipped school the day before the prom decorating was to begin to finish one of the largest murals.

Needless to say, I ended up with painful, bulging blisters on the tips of each of my fingers by the time prom night rolled around. But my Junior Prom turned out to be a painful experience that went way beyond my throbbing fingertips.

My parents were right in the middle of getting their divorce in May of 1965, and my mother was supposed to be one of the chaperones that night. I was looking forward to her coming too, because my high school boyfriend, Jay, and I were one of six couples nominated to be the prom "Prince and Princess." (At Dyer Central's proms, the king and queen were chosen from the Senior Class and the prince and princes from the hosting Junior Class.)

But shortly before Jay was scheduled to pick me up that evening, my father unexpectedly showed up "to take pictures," he said. He'd been drinking again, and with his usual intimidating flair managed to upset my mother, who then backed out of chaperoning. She was a sobbing mess. I was a blubbering basketcase. I think my dog, Beauty, was even howling by the time he left. What should have been my perfect dream night had turned into a nightmare.

Mom managed to redo my makeup. I wore long, white gloves to cover my blistered hands. Thankfully, Jay was late. Exhausted like the rest of us — including an "unknown" classmate who'd shot out one of the gym lights with his bee-bee gun because "it ruined the ambiance" — it seemed Jay had fallen asleep in his car.

He never knew of the emotional roller coaster ride I'd been on before his arrival when he stretched the elastic band to place a beautiful red and white carnation wrist corsage over my gloved hand. I mentally breathed a sigh of relief that he didn't have to pin the flowers on my chest.

When the winners of the evening's royalty were announced, Jay squeezed my hand so tightly it brought tears to my eyes. That momentary grasp, however, didn't hurt half as much as the pain of not having my mother there to see me crowned the Junior Class Prom Princess.

The murals? They were a great success. The prom photographer asked to purchase them to use as backdrops for future proms.

My blistered hands? They recovered, none the worse for wear.

The ache in my heart from the emotional scars as a child of an ugly divorce. At times, it still throbs today.

This morning's encounter with the silhouetted fishermen on Lake Manitou has again drawn me to the poignant memories of yesterday. But not unlike the radiant blend of colors of the sky, I can now see God's handiwork in even the pain of life. For I know He's been the patient, all-knowing artist of my life story, and even today, is still blending the joys and sorrows into a masterpiece of His own making.

There has never been the slightest doubt in my mind that the God who started this great work in you would keep at it and bring it to a flourishing finish on the day Christ Jesus appears.

Philippians 1:6 (TM)

I Worship You

The heavens proclaim his righteousness, and all the peoples see his glory.
Psalm 97:6 (ESV)

I was born to sing a new song, and in lifting my voice, I worship You.

I was born to dance a grand ballet, and in spinning my pirouettes, I worship You.

I was born to write a best seller, and in penning my story,
I worship You.

I was born to giggle and laugh, and in sharing my smile,
I worship You.

I was born to march a parade, and in strutting my joy, I worship You.

I was born to pedal my bike, and in the rhythm of the journey, I worship You.

I was born to customize beauty, and in fashioning my handiwork, I worship you.

I was born to teach a small child, and in motivating excellence, I worship You.

I was born to grow in grace, and in humbling myself, I worship You.

I was born to love and be loved, and in offering my life, I worship You.

The Golden Ring

To see life thru a child's eyes,
The Holy Scriptures say,
Dream fearlessly—take time to find
The wonder in each day:

The sparrow's hymn, a baby's grin,
The majesty of trees,
Nymph butterflies, the gold sunrise,
Parades of honking geese . . .

Reject the world's opinion that
It's time to "Act your age!"
You know, deep in your knower,
That today's your only stage.

You may not get the chance
to dance tomorrow's minuet,
So commandeer the moment
With a triple pirouette!

To give your all. Your everything!
To seize the golden ring,
Placed within the grasp of children
Who still live to please The King.

Contributing Authors

MICHELLE MEDLOCK ADAMS is a best-selling author of over 100 books and is Chairman of the Board of Advisors for Serious Writer, Inc, an online instructor for the Serious Writer Academy, owner and editor of "Wren & Bear Books," and a much sought-after speaker at professional writing conferences and women's retreats all over the United States. https://michellemedlockadams.com https://www.facebook.com › IN-writergirl~ Shall We Dance?

MARTHA BOLTON was Bob Hope's first female staff writer, writing for his television specials, personal appearances, and military shows for approximately fifteen years. An Emmy nominee, Dove Award nominee, and WGA Award nominee, she co-authored *DEAR BOB . . . Bob Hope's Wartime Correspondence with the G.I.s of WWII* and is a playwright for a dozen musicals currently playing in three states. https://www.amazon.com/stores/author/B001ITTK0S/about ~ Caboose Crossroads ~One-On-One with Mom ~ Thanks For The Memories

CRYSTAL BOWMAN is an award-winning, best-selling author of more than 100 books for children and families including devotions, board books, holidays, and books for women. She also writes lyrics for children's piano music and stories for *Clubhouse Jr.* magazine. https://crystalbowm an.com/ ctystaljbowman@gmail.com ~ Adventure in the Rainforest

DAWN SCOTT DAMON is a Pastor, and Best-Selling, Award-winning Author, National Speaker, Podcaster, and Founder of The Brave New Dawn and "The BraveHearted Woman," a transformational coaching and personal growth enterprise. Dawn travels throughout the USA speaking, teaching, and changing lives.http://dawnscottdamon.com/ dawn@brave heartedwoman.com ~ Perfect Timing

PAM FARRELL and her husband Bill are prolific conference and church communicators who speak at marriage and parenting conferences with a unique ability to "speak as one." She's published more than 40 books including the best-seller *Men are like Waffles, Women are Like Spaghetti.* Contact her at pamelafarrel@gmail.com ~ May I Have This Dance?

BARRY FRISINGER, an avid golfer, taught public school music for 44 years where his bands won numerous state and national titles. Today he plays first chair trumpet in The Grace College Wind Ensemble, the Lake Area Community Band, and participates in the Symphony of The Lakes Orchestra in Warsaw, IN. https://www.facebook.com/barry.frisinger.3/ bdfrisinger@gmail.com ~One Stroke At A Time

JUDY HARTZELL writes biographical historical works, publishing two books about her Mayo Clinic family, a series of articles about children's author Meindert DeJong, and just completed a book of 60 haiku poems with photos. Contact Judy at checkmatejt@gmail.com ~ Skinny-Dipping Lamentation

SHARON JAYNES is an international conference speaker and best-selling author of 25 books. For ten years, she served as vice-president of Proverbs 31 Ministries, and is co-founder of "Girlfriends in God." https://sharo njaynes.com/about/ sharon@sharonjaynes.com ~ The Lame Man Who Taught Me To Dance

LAURA KAY LOVEBERRY energizes audiences nationwide as an inspirational speaker. She writes books encouraging women with wit and wisdom. At school presentations, Laura's 3-minute caricatures and art books delight children. https://www.lauraloveberry.com, loveberrylk@gmail.com ~ Panty Hose Ribbon Dance

AMBER WEIGAND-BUCKLEY is the multi-award-winning founding editor/art director of *LEADING HEARTS* magazine, the official voice of the Advanced Writers and Speakers Association (AWSA). Specializing in Global Brand and Communications Management, she's had over 200 published works. barefacedjourney@gmail.com   https://www.linkedin.com ~ Groovers, Movers and Rollers

AMANDA FORSTER SCHAEFER is an author and works at A Cup of Gratitude Podcast and Bible Teacher, Author, and Speaker https://podcasts.apple.com/us/podcast/a-cup-of-gratitude/id1550450613~Dancing In The Eye Of The Storm

ONE CHANCE...ONE DANCE

Don't Miss the Moments of Your Life

No one can dance your unique life-dance but you.

I scrub my hands with purest soap, then join hands with the others in the great circle, dancing around your altar, God, singing God-songs at the top of my lungs, telling God-stories.
Psalm 26:6-7 (TM)

Donna Frisinger
Award-Winning-Author
Inspirational Speaker

"Twenty years from now you will be more disappointed by the things you didn't do than by the ones you did do."
Mark Twain

If you have forgotten the spontaneous pirouette of your childhood, isn't it time to go looking for it? To let go of anything that has crippled your desire to swirl, twirl and whirl before the King? Bitterness. Disappointments. Failures...No matter, God is the God of second, third, umpteenth chances. Life is waaay too short, and it's never too late to dig out those old dancing shoes to boogie to the beat of the song God Himself planted in your heart the day He created you.

Donna has invested her life in teaching others to dance, both literally and figuratively. Told she had two left feet early in life, she went on to be captain of both her high school and college dance teams. Named "Indiana's Dance Educator of the Year," she was co-founder of the IHSDTA (Indiana High School Dance Team Association), ran her own Fine Arts Academy, and produced Broadway-style church musicals. Her groups consistently won state and national championships while learning invaluable life lessons along the way.

Continue the Connection

www.donnafrisinger.com
bdfrisinger@gmail.com

SCAN ME

Endorsements

- Michelle Medlock Adams
- Linda Evans Shepherd
- Lee Ann Mancini
- Karen Whiting
- Blythe Daniel
- Pam Farrel
- Susan Neal
- Carol Kent

Most Recent Writing Awards

- 2022 AWSA Golden Scroll Recipient
- 2020 1st Place Golden Scroll
- 2020 SILVER Illumination Award
- 2020 BRONZE Illumination Award
- 2019 1st Place Texas Book Festival

As a freelancer, Donna's published in *Clubhouse, Clubhouse Jr., Mature Living, Today's Christian Woman, Ideals, War Cry, Guidepost Books, Christian Communicator, American Legion, Marriage Partnership, On Course, Power for Living, Indiana AHPERD Journal, Indiana Federation of Poetry,* and *several anthologies.*